D0618287

At Issue

| Racial Profiling

Other books in the At Issue series:

Antidepressants

Are America's Wealthy Too Powerful?

Are Conspiracy Theories Valid?

Are Privacy Rights Being Violated?

Child Sexual Abuse

Creationism Versus Evolution

Does Outsourcing Harm America?

Does the World Hate the United States?

Do Nuclear Weapons Pose a Serious Threat?

Drug Testing

The Ethics of Genetic Engineering

The Ethics of Human Cloning

Gay and Lesbian Families

Gay Marriage

Gene Therapy

How Can Domestic Violence Be Prevented?

How Does Religion Influence Politics?

Hurricane Katrina

Is American Society Too Materialistic?

Is the Mafia Still a Force in America?

Is Poverty a Serious Threat?

Legalizing Drugs

Prescription Drugs

Responding to the AIDS Epidemic

School Shootings

Steroids

What Causes Addiction?

At Issue

Racial Profiling

Kris Hirschmann, Book Editor

GREENHAVEN PRESS

An imprint of Thomson Gale, a part of The Thomson Corporation

Detroit • New York • San Francisco • New Haven, Conn. • Waterville, Maine • London • Munich

Bonnie Szumski, *Publisher*
Helen Cothran, *Managing Editor*

© 2006 Thomson Gale, a part of The Thomson Corporation.

Thomson and Star Logo are trademarks and Gale and Greenhaven Press are registered trademarks used herein under license.

For more information, contact:
Greenhaven Press
27500 Drake Rd.
Farmington Hills, MI 48331-3535
Or you can visit our Internet site at http://www.gale.com

Cover photograph reproduced by permission of David McNew/Getty Images.

LIBRARY OF CONGRESS CATALOGING-IN-PUBLICATION DATA

Racial Profiling / Kris Hirschmann, editor.
    p. cm. -- (At issue)
    Includes bibliographical references and index.
    ISBN 0-7377-1980-X (alk. paper) -- ISBN 0-7377-1979-6 (alk. paper)
    1. Racial profiling in law enforcement. 2. Minorities--Civil rights. I. Hirschmann, Kris, 1967– II. At issue (San Diego, Calif.)
    HV7936.R3R325 2007
    363.2'3089--dc22

                                        2006043375

Printed in the United States of America
10 9 8 7 6 5 4 3 2 1

Contents

Introduction   7

1. U.S. Policies Forbid Racial Profiling   10

   U.S. Department of Justice, Civil Rights Division

2. U.S. Policies Sanction Racial Profiling   16

   American Civil Liberties Union

3. Profiling Muslims Is Essential in the War on Terror   21

   Andrew C. McCarthy

4. Profiling Muslims Hinders the War on Terror   27

   Leadership Conference on Civil Rights Education Fund

5. Airlines Should Screen Passengers Who Match Terrorists' Racial Profiles   35

   Stuart Taylor Jr.

6. Airlines Should Use Behavioral Profiling, Not Racial Profiling   42

   Bruce Schneier

7. The Benefits of Racial Profiling Justify Some Loss of Civil Liberties   46

   Robert A. Levy

8. The Benefits of Racial Profiling Cannot Justify Any Loss of Civil Liberties   51

   Christina Fauchon

9. All Police Officers Practice Racial Profiling   57

   Fred Reed

10. Racial Profiling in Law Enforcement Is a Myth   62

   Heather Mac Donald

11. Racial Profiling Is Useful if Properly Regulated   71

   Peter H. Schuck

12. U.S. Racial Profiling Policies Are Based on   78
    Political Correctness, Not Logic
    Michelle Malkin
13. Racial Profiling Has a Heavy Social Cost   83
    Amnesty International
14. Racial Profiling Undermines the U.S.   92
    Legal System
    David A. Harris

Organizations to Contact   101
Bibliography   107
Index   111

Introduction

On the morning of September 11, 2001, terrorists seized control of four commercial airplanes in the northeastern United States. Two of the airplanes were deliberately crashed into the Twin Towers of the World Trade Center in New York City. Another was flown into the Pentagon in Washington, D.C. The fourth plane went down in a Pennsylvania field after passengers struggled with the hijackers. Including the airplanes' passengers, these attacks killed about three thousand people—the deadliest act of terrorism ever to occur on U.S. soil.

In the days and weeks following the attacks, a stunned United States tried to make sense of what had happened. Investigators quickly discovered that nineteen hijackers had been involved in what came to be called 9/11. They were all young male Muslims of Arab descent. The hijackers were linked to a radical Islamist organization called al Qaeda, which had publicly announced a jihad (holy war) against the United States. "Terrorizing you, while you are carrying arms in our land, is a legitimate and morally demanded duty. . . . It is a duty now on every tribe in the Arab Peninsula to fight Jihad in the cause of Allah," al Qaeda leader Osama bin Laden had declared in 1996.

It was clear that the attacks of 9/11 were not the acts of a few desperate men. The United States was at war, and radical Islam was the opponent. Stunned by this revelation, people all over the United States began to demand protection. Many of these people reasoned that because the attacks of 9/11 had been carried out by Muslims, the U.S. government should focus its terrorism-prevention efforts on Muslims and/or Middle Easterners. This type of racial profiling—singling out individuals for special scrutiny solely because of their ethnicity—would surely detect and stop any would-be terrorists.

Profiling in War

Racial profiling in wartime is not a new idea. In the United States, this tactic had been used extensively after Japan's 1941 attack on Pearl Harbor during World War II. Shortly after the attack, officials decided that Japanese nationals and even Japanese Americans who lived on the West Coast might be a threat to national security. As a result, many of these people were forced to leave their homes and live in internment camps, where they could be watched closely for signs of disloyalty.

The vast majority of the 120,000 people caught up in the Japanese American internment program had done nothing wrong or even suspicious. Their only crime was looking Japanese. But the Japanese threat was considered severe enough to justify any hardship these people might experience. This sentiment was summed up by General John DeWitt, who supervised the internment program. "There is no way to determine their loyalty. . . . It makes no difference whether [a person] is an American citizen, he is still a Japanese," DeWitt testified before Congress.

Profiling in Peace

In peacetime, too, the United States has had plenty of experience with racial profiling. The most prominent example of peacetime profiling is the extra attention (invariably negative) that police officers are alleged to pay to black Americans. According to some people, there is a belief in the law enforcement community that blacks are more likely to break the law than whites, Hispanics, or people of other ethnicities. As a result, police officers may detain blacks more often than people of other races.

No one can prove exactly how much racial profiling goes on in law enforcement. Surveys show that black Americans, however, are almost uniformly convinced that this practice is common today. The phenomenon has even acquired a nickname: "driving while black." This term is a play on the phrase "driving while intoxicated." It implies that drivers may be considered suspicious simply because they have dark skin.

An Ongoing Debate

Public opinions about racial profiling have changed over the decades. During World War II, for instance, many Americans thought it was a good idea to detain people of Japanese descent. Today, however, attitudes have shifted, and the internment of Japanese Americans is usually described as a shameful blotch on America's history. In 1988, the U.S. government even issued a formal apology to internment survivors and their descendants, acknowledging that the episode was based on "race prejudice, war hysteria, and a failure of political leadership."

Attitudes toward racial profiling in law enforcement have changed as well. From the post slavery decades after the Civil War to the 1950s, most white Americans thought it was perfectly acceptable to treat black people differently from white people. As the nation moved toward a more egalitarian and race-blind philosophy, however, this view fell out of favor. By the late 1990s, the federal government was passing laws against racial profiling, and police departments all over the nation were training their staff accordingly.

It was into this atmosphere that the 9/11 bomb dropped. The debate on racial profiling, which had virtually burned out, was suddenly hot again. The big question was whether the United States should permit or encourage the profiling of Muslims and Middle Easterners. To some people, this practice seemed like the only logical response to 9/11. Others were strongly opposed for a wide variety of reasons, both practical and ideological. The debate began to rage anew—and it is still raging today.

1

U.S. Policies Forbid Racial Profiling

U.S. Department of Justice, Civil Rights Division

The United States Department of Justice is the nation's central agency for the enforcement of federal laws. The Civil Rights Division is responsible for enforcing federal statutes that prohibit discrimination on the basis of race, sex, handicap, religion, and national origin.

The use of racial profiling as a law enforcement tool is detrimental both to individuals and to the United States as a whole. For this reason, official U.S. policies forbid the practice. Law enforcement officers may not consider race or ethnicity unless they have a detailed suspect description that indicates race or trustworthy information that links persons of a certain race to a crime. Moreover, in national security matters, officials may consider race only to the extent permitted by the nation's laws and the Constitution. These guidelines provide ample protection against racial profiling abuses.

In his February 27, 2001, Address to a Joint Session of Congress, President George W. Bush declared that racial profiling is "wrong and we will end it in America." He directed the Attorney General [John Ashcroft] to review the use by

U.S. Dept. of Justice, "Guidance Regarding the Use of Race by Federal Law Enforcement Agencies," www.usdoj.gov, June 2003. Reproduced by permission.

Federal law enforcement authorities of race as a factor in conducting stops, searches and other law enforcement investigative procedures. The Attorney General, in turn, instructed the Civil Rights Division to develop guidance for Federal officials to ensure an end to racial profiling in law enforcement. . . .

The use of race as the basis for law enforcement decision-making clearly has a terrible cost, both to the individuals who suffer invidious discrimination and to the Nation, whose goal of "liberty and justice for all" recedes with every act of such discrimination. For this reason, this guidance in many cases imposes more restrictions on the consideration of race and ethnicity in Federal law enforcement than the Constitution requires. This guidance prohibits racial profiling in law enforcement practices without hindering the important work of our Nation's public safety officials, particularly the intensified anti-terrorism efforts precipitated by the events of September 11, 2001. . . .

Guidance for Federal Law Enforcement

Domestic Law Enforcement. In making routine or spontaneous law enforcement decisions, such as ordinary traffic stops, Federal law enforcement officers may not use race or ethnicity to any degree, except that officers may rely on race and ethnicity in a specific suspect description. This prohibition applies even where the use of race or ethnicity might otherwise be lawful.

Federal law enforcement agencies and officers sometimes engage in law enforcement activities, such as traffic and foot patrols, that generally do not involve either the ongoing investigation of specific criminal activities or the prevention of catastrophic events or harm to the national security. Rather, their activities are typified by spontaneous action in response to the activities of individuals whom they happen to encounter in the course of their patrols and about whom they have no information other than their observations. These general enforcement responsibilities should be carried out without *any* consideration of race or ethnicity. . . .

The President has made clear his concern that racial profiling is morally wrong and inconsistent with our core values and principles of fairness and justice.

Racial Profiling Must Not Occur

Some have argued that overall discrepancies in certain crime rates among racial groups could justify using race as a factor in general traffic enforcement activities and would produce a greater number of arrests for non-traffic offenses (*e.g.*, narcotics trafficking). We emphatically reject this view. The President has made clear his concern that racial profiling is morally wrong and inconsistent with our core values and principles of fairness and justice. Even if there were overall statistical evidence of differential rates of commission of certain offenses among particular races, the affirmative use of such generalized notions by Federal law enforcement officers in routine, spontaneous law enforcement activities is tantamount to stereotyping. It casts a pall of suspicion over every member of certain racial and ethnic groups without regard to the specific circumstances of a particular investigation or crime, and it offends the dignity of the individual improperly targeted. Whatever the motivation, it is patently unacceptable and thus prohibited under this guidance for Federal law enforcement officers to act on the belief that race or ethnicity signals a higher risk of criminality. This is the core of "racial profiling" and it must not occur.

The situation is different when an officer has specific information, based on trustworthy sources, to "be on the lookout" for specific individuals identified at least in part by race or ethnicity. In such circumstances, the officer is not acting based on a generalized assumption about persons of different races; rather, the officer is helping locate specific individuals previously identified as involved in crime. . . .

Reliance upon generalized stereotypes is absolutely forbidden.

Law Enforcement in Specific Investigations. In conducting activities in connection with a specific investigation, Federal law enforcement officers may consider race and ethnicity only to the extent that there is trustworthy information, relevant to the locality or time frame, that links persons of a particular race or ethnicity to an identified criminal incident, scheme, or organization. This standard applies even where the use of race or ethnicity might otherwise be lawful.

As noted above, there are circumstances in which law enforcement activities relating to particular identified criminal incidents, schemes or enterprises may involve consideration of personal identifying characteristics of potential suspects, including age, sex, ethnicity or race. Common sense dictates that when a victim describes the assailant as being of a particular race, authorities may properly limit their search for suspects to persons of that race. Similarly, in conducting an ongoing investigation into a specific criminal organization whose membership has been identified as being overwhelmingly of one ethnicity, law enforcement should not be expected to disregard such facts in pursuing investigative leads into the organization's activities.

Reliance upon generalized stereotypes is absolutely forbidden. Rather, use of race or ethnicity is permitted only when the officer is pursuing a specific lead concerning the identifying characteristics of persons involved in an *identified* criminal activity. . . .

Threats to National Security or Borders

In investigating or preventing threats to national security or other catastrophic events (including the performance of duties related to air transportation security), or in enforcing laws protecting the integrity of the Nation's borders, Federal law enforcement officers may not consider race or ethnicity except to the extent permitted by the Constitution and laws of the United States.

Constitutional provisions limiting government action on the basis of race are wide-ranging and provide substantial protections at every step of the investigative and judicial process.

Since the terrorist attacks on September 11, 2001, the President has emphasized that Federal law enforcement personnel must use every legitimate tool to prevent future attacks, protect our Nation's borders, and deter those who would cause devastating harm to our Nation and its people through the use of biological or chemical weapons, other weapons of mass destruction, suicide hijackings, or any other means. . . .

The Constitution prohibits consideration of race or ethnicity in law enforcement decisions in all but the most exceptional instances. Given the incalculably high stakes involved in such investigations, however, Federal law enforcement officers who are protecting national security or preventing catastrophic events (as well as airport security screeners) may consider race, ethnicity, and other relevant factors to the extent permitted by our laws and the Constitution. Similarly, because enforcement of the laws protecting the Nation's borders may necessarily involve a consideration of a person's alienage in certain circumstances, the use of race or ethnicity in such circumstances is properly governed by existing statutory and constitutional standards. . . .

Existing Laws Are Effective

In sum, constitutional provisions limiting government action on the basis of race are wide-ranging and provide substantial protections at every step of the investigative and judicial process. Accordingly. . .when addressing matters of national security, border integrity, or the possible catastrophic loss of life, existing legal and constitutional standards are an appropriate guide for Federal law enforcement officers.

2

U.S. Policies Sanction Racial Profiling

American Civil Liberties Union

The mission of the American Civil Liberties Union is to defend and preserve the rights and freedoms guaranteed by the U.S. Constitution and the laws of the United States. The organization does this work through legal action, live testimony, written reports and position papers, and many other avenues.

Proof exists that racial profiling is both inefficient and ineffective, both domestically and in counterterrorism efforts. Officially, the federal guidelines on the use of racial profiling in law enforcement (spelled out in the government document "Guidance Regarding the Use of Race by Federal Law Enforcement Agencies") forbid using race or ethnicity to identify crime suspects. In reality, the guidelines fall far short of this standard. They do not have the force of law, and most significantly, they exempt national security efforts. To address this problem, Congress should act quickly to pass the End Racial Profiling Act of 2001.

On June 17, 2003 President [George W.] Bush publicly released a set of guidelines promulgated by the Civil Rights Division of the Department of Justice entitled, *Regard-*

ing the Use of Race by Federal Law Enforcement Agencies. The introduction to the guidelines alluded to the president's February 2001 address to Congress in which he declared that racial profiling is "wrong and we will end it in America." The accompanying Fact Sheet on Racial Profiling issued by the Department of Justice contains phrases like:

- "racial profiling is wrong and will not be tolerated;"
- "America has a moral obligation to prohibit racial profiling;" and
- "stereotyping certain races as having a greater propensity to commit crimes is absolutely prohibited."

But the guidelines themselves fall far short of the Bush administration's rhetorical posturing. Since they are only a set of guidelines, rather than a law or an executive order, they have no teeth. They acknowledge racial profiling as a national concern, but they provide no enforcement mechanisms or methods for tracking whether or not federal law enforcement agencies are in compliance.

The guidelines' most serious flaw, however, is that they carve out a huge national security loophole. The guidelines specify:

> The above standards do not affect current Federal policy with respect to law enforcement activities and other efforts to defend and safeguard against threats to national security or the integrity of the Nation's borders. . . .

Only through federal legislation can the problem of racial profiling be comprehensively identified and ended.

Since the 9/11 terrorist attacks, it has been the official policy of the United States government to stop, interrogate and detain individuals without criminal charge—often for long periods of time on the basis of their national origin, ethnicity and religion. In fact, the very inclusion of a national security exception in the guidelines is an admission by the Department of Justice that it relies upon racial and ethnic profiling in its domestic counterterrorism efforts.

Pass the End Racial Profiling Act

In response to the severe shortcomings in the president's guidelines, a bipartisan group of lawmakers in both the House of Representatives and the Senate has introduced the "End Racial Profiling Act," a comprehensive package designed to track and provide steps toward eliminating racial, ethnic, religious and national origin profiling. As this report went to print [in February 2004] nearly 100 members of Congress had co-sponsored the measure and a large coalition of public advocates from many points on the political spectrum, including several law enforcement organizations, were actively working to ensure it receives its due consideration in Washington. [As of mid-2006, the bill was awaiting action by the Senate Justice Committee.]

Specifically, the bill would define racial, ethnic, religious and national origin profiling, ban their use and provide a cause of action for individuals harmed by these forms of profiling. It would permit the attorney general to withhold funds from non-compliant police departments and government agencies and would provide grants to aid compliance. And, crucially, it would require data collection to ensure police accountability and provide police executives with a needed management tool.

Congress should act expediently to make this legislation law. Only through federal legislation can the problem of racial profiling be comprehensively identified and ended. . . .

Racial Profiling Is Inefficient, Ineffective

The ACLU [American Civil Liberties Union] opposes all racial, religious and ethnic profiling, whether in the context of routine law enforcement, or domestic counterterrorism. As we have argued repeatedly in our litigation, legislative advocacy and public statements over the years, racial profiling is in every instance inconsistent with this country's core constitutional principles of equality and fairness.

We have also argued that law enforcement based on general characteristics such as race, religion and national origin, rather than on the observation of an individual's behavior, is an inefficient and ineffective strategy for ensuring public safety. The strength of this argument has been borne out over and over again by data that has been collected by individual police departments throughout the country in response to ACLU lawsuits and the public's demands for answers and police accountability.

We now have incontrovertible proof that racial profiling does not, in fact, give the police a "leg up" in fighting crime. The premise upon which it is based—that certain ethnic minorities are more likely than whites to be in violation of the law—is simply wrong. Studies consistently show that "hit rates"—the discovery of contraband or evidence of other illegal conduct—among minorities stopped and searched by the police are lower than "hit rates" for whites who are stopped and searched. Indeed, the findings of numerous studies throughout the country have been so consistent that police officials are starting to recognize that racial profiling, while still practiced broadly, is ineffective and should be rejected. . . .

There is no reason to believe that a counterterrorism strategy based on ethnic profiling will be any more effective. The overwhelming majority of Muslims, Middle Easterners and South Asians are hardworking, law-abiding people. Singling them out for special law enforcement scrutiny will produce the same low "hit rates" as has racial profiling in the context of drug law enforcement. . . .

An Illogical Approach

But in spite of the overwhelming evidence that racial profiling is counterproductive, and in spite of the counsel of intelligence experts that the better method for identifying potential terrorists is through observation of "pre-attack" behaviors, [former U.S.] Attorney General John Ashcroft immediately launched a counterterrorism strategy that centers on profiling based on national origin. Moreover, even as it became obvious that the strategy was not producing results, the attorney general continued to conceive and implement increasingly grandiose schemes based on ethnic profiling. These are the "activities and other efforts" President Bush has exempted from his guidelines.

3

Profiling Muslims Is Essential in the War on Terror

Andrew C. McCarthy

Former federal prosecutor Andrew C. McCarthy is currently a senior fellow at the conservative Foundation for the Defense of Democracies and a contributor to the National Review.

Terrorists are mostly young Muslim males of Middle Eastern descent. Although this fact is clear not only from the attacks of September 11, 2001, but also from subsequent events, the U.S. government refuses to acknowledge it. This attitude defies common sense. Profiling may be distasteful, but it is perfectly constitutional—and indeed, using this tool is the government's duty when a specific ethnic or religious group poses a serious threat to U.S. security. In the past, law enforcement officials have successfully used ethnic profiles to pursue race-based criminal organizations. Today, however, the government seems to be queasy about using this approach. As a result, airport and subway searches are ridiculously ineffective. By refusing to face reality, the United States is virtually inviting terrorists to attack again.

Year four of the War on Terror is coming to a close with the [July 2005] bombing of London's mass-transit system by Islamist terrorists. Year three saw the Islamists bomb

Madrid's railway, as well as synagogues, businesses, and the British consulate in Istanbul. In year two, they struck a resort in Kenya, nightclubs in Bali, and Western citizens in Casablanca and Riyadh. And in year one, even as we waged a massive counterattack in the aftermath of [the terrorist attacks of September 11, 2001], they managed to savage a synagogue in Tunisia.

There is a pattern here—but the U.S. government seems to be incapable of detecting it. We have met the enemy, and it is militant Islam. Yet we refuse to acknowledge that fact, pretending that the enemy is "terror"—a method of attack—rather than the terrorists who employ that method. The latest expression of our refusal to identify the enemy is our ongoing debate over "racial profiling." One cannot listen to this debate without wondering whether three decades of political correctness have undermined not only the common sense necessary for survival, but our will to survive itself.

Terrorists Have a Profile

I was on a panel some months ago with a top official from the Department of Homeland Security. After reeling off three now-infamous but manifestly non-Arabic names—Richard Reid (the "Shoe Bomber"), John Walker Lindh (the "American Taliban"), and Jose Padilla (allegedly a would-be "Dirty Bomber")—the official offered to that room full of idealistic law students the cheery lesson our government has drawn: You can't construct a terrorist profile because the monsters come in all colors, shapes, and sizes. As I listened to this absurdity, I couldn't help but think of Muggsy Bogues, the five-foot-three-inch dynamo of a point guard who lit up pro-basketball arenas for years. I hope that if some exigency ever impels the Transportation Safety Administration [TSA] to put together an NBA team, the agency will not think "Muggsy" and scour the land for Lilliputians.

Terrorists—particularly those who are likely to attack—have a profile. They are Muslim males, overwhelmingly young adults of Middle Eastern and North African descent. That doesn't mean everyone who falls into that profile is a terrorist. Nor does it mean that every terrorist will fit the profile—you will get the occasional Reid, Lindh, or Padilla. But so what? A profile is not a judgment of guilt. It is not even an accusation of guilt. It is an investigative tool. It enables law enforcement to organize suspicions and husband resources rationally, in a manner related to a known threat. It is not foolproof, but no one who utilizes it is under any such misimpression. Its point is not to cast aspersions but to improve the odds of thwarting an attack the fallout of which could be catastrophic. It is essential in any strategy aimed at preventing a strike rather than prosecuting the guilty after the victims have been slaughtered.

The Constitution . . . is not a suicide pact. If a profound threat stems from a particular group, the government may take that fact into account.

Racial Profiling Is Constitutional

Profiling is not congenial to our tender postmodern sensibilities. Nonetheless, it is legally inoffensive, at least under federal law. To be sure, the Fourteenth Amendment guarantees all persons equal protection. Yet this has never meant anything so absurd as that government must in all circumstances regard everyone as the same. The state routinely, and quite properly, makes commonsense distinctions: A seven-foot-tall naval officer may be ruled ineligible for duty in the tight confines of a submarine; women are excluded from combat missions; members of both sexes may be barred from employment as firemen or police officers if unable to meet physical-strength criteria; and so on.

Moreover, if the state interest at issue is compelling enough, even suspect distinctions such as those based on race or ethnicity are permissible. The Supreme Court has recently held that states may use race and ethnicity as grounds for denying qualified Americans admission to universities—and for no better reason than to achieve a critical mass of student diversity. How much more compelling is our interest in saving lives?

The Supreme Court has long recognized the security of the governed as the highest imperative of government. The Constitution, as Justice Robert Jackson famously observed, is not a suicide pact. If a profound threat stems from a particular group, the government may take that fact into account when deciding how to marshal its resources. The government has no less than a duty to do so, and until recently this duty was carried out without much controversy.

It has, for example, been established federal law since the Alien Enemies Act of 1798 that, in a time of declared war, the United States may imprison or deport nationals of enemy nations. (What was excessive about internment camps during the Second World War was that they included American citizens of Japanese descent; there was nothing objectionable in principle about holding Japanese, German, or Italian nationals.) In the War on Terror, the enemy is a global network rather than a nation—but that complication hardly extinguishes the underlying principle: Those whose allegiance may lie with the enemy must be subject to greater scrutiny.

A History of Success

This line of thinking is not exclusive to wartime considerations. The Mafia has historically been a syndicate composed of males of Italian descent. In the prosecutions of the 1980s and 1990s that shattered the mob, the Justice Department did not cast its net widely enough to snare octogenarian Guatemalan grannies; it made Italian heritage part of the profile. Likewise, the

Westies were a Hell's Kitchen–based Irish mob; in dismantling it, the government did not target, well, Muggsy Bogues. Ditto for Chinese tongs, Colombian drug cartels, Russian organized crime, Nigerian scammers, and the entire gorgeous mosaic of crime.

Criminal conspiracies, like much concerted activity (including much that is socially beneficial), tend to be ethnic and cultural. Government was never expected to ignore that reality when the worst consequence of misdirected attention might have been a gang murder or a kilo of cocaine slipping into the stream of narcotics traffic. Why would anyone think the blinders should go on when the consequence could be mass homicide—tens or hundreds of thousands of deaths—in a WMD [weapons of mass destruction] attack?

Ineffective Screening

Our chariness about profiling is best seen in post-9/11 airport procedures and, following the London tube bombings, in New York City's subway searches. As to the former, one sees its absurdity by imagining an international network of old ladies intent on carrying out suicide strikes. Does anyone think the TSA would have the nerve to subject young Muslims to aggressive secondary screening at the nation's airports? Yet, in our current war against militant Muslims, no one—not children, not aged invalids—is immune from overwrought intrusion, lest we be thought inhospitable to the genus exclusively within which lies the barbaric species aiming to destroy us.

The NYPD's subway searches, meanwhile, are ludicrously benign. To forfend claims of profiling, the cops are reacting to militant Islam's atrocities by randomly stopping approximately every tenth person carrying a bag. (Query: Why is it kosher to discriminate against bag-carriers? Don't they have a lobby?) Further underscoring that this is a gesture, not a strategy, the police announce their presence at a particular station ahead of time; real bombers need only tote their bags a few blocks to the next stop. And no one who has the misfortune of being stopped is forced to undergo a search—if you object to opening your knapsack, the police will leave you alone, although you will not be permitted to board a train. No profiling, no searches, and no effectiveness.

Yet the NYPD is still being sued by the New York Civil Liberties Union. NYCLU's complaint, after mouthing that "concerns about terrorism of course justify—indeed, require—aggressive police tactics," argues that the searches violate the Constitution because they lack individualized suspicion. It then argues that they could easily lead to such suspicion, and to profiling—which would, conveniently, also violate the Constitution.

An Invitation to Strike Again

This attempt to have it both ways, consistency be damned, is lunacy run amok. In fact, *not* focusing on those who pose a danger is flagrantly to violate civil rights: specifically, the right of the vast majority of Americans to be free from unreasonable searches.

Which is to say nothing of the right to life of everyone we are failing to protect. Until we stop pretending not to see what the terrorists who are attacking us look like, we may as well give them an engraved invitation to strike again.

4

Profiling Muslims Hinders the War on Terror

Leadership Conference on Civil Rights Education Fund

The Leadership Conference on Civil Rights Education Fund (LCCREF) is the education and research arm of the Leadership Conference on Civil Rights. The goal of LCCREF is to promote understanding of the need for national policies that support civil rights and social and economic justice and to encourage an appreciation of the nation's diversity. To this end, LCCREF has produced educational materials, special reports, briefings, and curricula on a wide variety of civil rights issues.

Advocates of racial profiling reason that terrorists are most likely to belong to certain racial, ethnic, or religious groups. However, many examples prove that this assumption is false. Not only is racial profiling unhelpful, it actually hinders *the antiterrorism effort by making it harder for law enforcement officials to investigate truly suspicious individuals. There are also several implementation problems with racial profiling. From a purely practical perspective, it can be impossible to correctly identify a person's race. Also, terrorists will change their techniques if they know officials are looking for people with certain characteristics.*

Leadership Conference on Civil Rights Education Fund, "Wrong Then, Wrong Now: Racial Profiling Before & After September 11, 2001," www.civilrights.org, February 27, 2003. Reproduced by permission.

And finally, profiling may upset and alienate people who are likely to identify terrorists. For all these reasons, racial profiling is an ineffective antiterrorism tactic.

The assumptions driving terrorism profiling are the same as those behind traditional, street-level profiling—i.e., that a particular crime (here, terrorism) is most likely to be committed by members of a particular racial, ethnic or religious group, and that members of that group are, in general, likely to be involved in that kind of criminal activity. . . .These assumptions are flawed.

First, it is not true that terrorist acts are necessarily perpetrated by Arabs, or that the perpetrator of a terrorist act is likely to be an Arab. While all the men involved in the September 11 hijackings were Arab nationals, Richard Reid, who on December 22, 2001, tried to ignite an explosive device on a trans-Atlantic flight, was a British citizen of Jamaican ancestry. Prior to September 11, the bloodiest act of terrorism on United States soil was perpetrated by [Oklahoma City bomber] Timothy McVeigh. Non-Arabs like John Walker Lindh can be found in the ranks of the Taliban, al Qaeda and other terrorist organizations. At the same time, the overwhelming majority of Arabs, Arab Americans, Muslims, South Asians and Sikhs are law-abiding persons who would never think of engaging in terrorism.

Profiling Hinders the Anti-Terrorism Effort

Focusing on the many Arabs, South Asians, Muslims, and Sikhs who clearly pose no threat to national security detracts from the anti-terrorism effort. First, it diverts precious law enforcement resources away from investigations of individuals—including Arabs and Muslims—who have been linked to terrorist activity by specific and credible evidence. Second, it ignores the possibility that someone who does not fit the profile may be engaged in terrorism, or may be an unwitting accomplice to terrorism.

That race is an ineffective measure of an individual's terrorist intentions was made clear in a memorandum circulated to American law enforcement agents worldwide by a group of senior U.S. law enforcement officials in October 2002. The memorandum, entitled "Assessing Behaviors," emphasized that focusing on the racial characteristics of individuals was a waste of law enforcement resources and might cause law enforcement officials to ignore suspicious behavior, past or present, by someone who did not fit a racial profile. One of the authors of the report noted: "Fundamentally, believing that you can achieve safety by looking at characteristics instead of behaviors is silly. If your goal is preventing attacks . . . you want your eyes and ears looking for pre-attack behaviors, not characteristics."

Any *emphasis on personal characteristics, rather than on behavior, misdirects scarce anti-terrorism resources.*

The memorandum urged investigators to focus on actual behavior involving selection of targets, recruitment and organization of members, acquisition of skills, assessing vulnerabilities of targets, acquiring financing, probing boundaries, communicating with conspirators, using insiders, maintaining secrecy, and acquiring weapons. An emphasis on race, the memorandum noted, distracts from the observance of potentially suspicious behavior. This memorandum answers one of the main arguments of those who support racial profiling in the context of airport searches—i.e., that it is simply logical to focus precious law enforcement resources on Arab men rather than on older women from Minnesota or Swedish au pairs. What U.S. intelligence experts have made clear is that *any* emphasis on personal characteristics, rather than on behavior, misdirects scarce anti-terrorism resources.

This is not to say that law enforcement can never rely on race in fighting terrorism. As in street-level law enforcement, it is permissible to rely on race as part of a suspect-specific description. No one argues, for example, that the police cannot follow up on a specific tip that a group of Arabs is plotting terrorist acts in a particular apartment building by questioning Arabs who live in that building. Assuming the reliability of the source or the specificity of the information, identification of an individual's race carries with it the real potential for uncovering criminal activity.

Racial profiling in any case is a crude mechanism; against an enemy like al Qaeda it is virtually useless.

Profiling, by contrast, is a scattershot device that is so crude as to be virtually useless. It is no coincidence that the questioning of 8,000 young Arab men in late 2001–early 2002 yielded virtually no leads about terrorism—there was no evidence to suggest that any of these men knew anything about terrorism in the first place.

Applying Racial Profiles Is Difficult

Racial profiling is particularly foolish in the anti-terrorism context for three additional reasons. First, even if one accepts the false assumption that terrorists are likely to be Arab or Muslim, the *application* of the profile is fraught with error . . . . Many persons who are neither Arab nor Muslim can get caught up in the terrorism profiling web. Consider these other examples from the airport security context:

- On October 22, 2001, four Hispanic businessmen were escorted off a Delta flight after passengers alerted airline staff that the men appeared to be Middle Eastern.

- On September 26, 2001, a group of six passengers of Indian ethnicity were questioned aboard a United Airlines flight from Los Angeles to Washington, D.C. The men were taken to the back of the plane, where they were first questioned by a pilot and then by FBI and INS [Immigration and Naturalization Service].

- On September 24, 2001, a Canadian woman of Indian origin was removed from her US Airways flight from Toronto to Las Vegas because her last name was similar in pronunciation to the name of one of the September 11 hijackers, Mohammed Atta. She was told that her name was "Middle Eastern" and therefore suspicious.

- A flight bound for New York's LaGuardia Airport was accompanied on its descent by a military plane after a passenger raised suspicions about a group of entertainers from India who were passing notes and changing seats. The group was detained for questioning and released five hours later without being charged. The passengers were not terrorists; they were animated because they were excited about visiting New York.

Thus, the profile of a terrorist as an Arab or Muslim has been applied to individuals who are neither Arab nor Muslim (e.g., Hispanics, Indians, and Sikhs). Profiling of Arabs and Muslims amounts to selective enforcement of the law against anyone with a certain type of "swarthy" foreign-looking appearance even if they do not in fact fit the terrorist profile. The profile is then useless in fighting terrorism, as well as offensive to an ever-broadening category of persons.

Terrorist Organizations Are Adaptable

Second, using racial profiling in the anti-terrorism effort is a classic example of refighting the last war. As noted above, al Qaeda and other terrorist organizations are pan-ethnic: they include Asians, Anglos, and ethnic Europeans. They are also adaptive, dynamic organizations that will learn how to use non-Arabs such as Richard Reid to carry out terrorist attacks, or to smuggle explosive devices onto planes in the luggage of innocent people. The fact that the September 11 hijackers were Arab means little in predicting who the next terrorists will be. Racial profiling in any case is a crude mechanism; against an enemy like al Qaeda it is virtually useless.

Profiling Alienates Possible Information Sources

Third, and perhaps most important, the use of profiling in the anti-terrorism context, as in the street-crime context, alienates the very people that federal authorities have deemed instrumental in the anti-terrorism fight. Arab, South Asian, and Muslim communities may yield useful information to those fighting terrorism. Arabs and Arab Americans also offer the government an important source of Arabic speakers and translators. The singling out of Arabs, South Asians, Muslims, and Sikhs for investigation regardless of whether any credible evidence links them to terrorism will simply alienate these individuals and compromise the anti-terrorism effort. In particular, to the extent that federal authorities use the anti-terrorism effort as a pretext for detaining or deporting immigration law violators, individuals who might have information that is useful against terrorism may be afraid to come forward. At a minimum, those individuals will choose not to register, thereby defeating the very purpose of the registration program.

The nation cannot afford to use an anti-terrorism mechanism as deeply flawed as racial profiling.

The alienation that results from terrorism profiling is compounded by the clumsy and insensitive manner in which it has thus far been carried out. . . . Arabs, South Asians, Muslims, and Sikhs who have tried to cooperate with authorities and to comply with the law have consistently been met by verbal (and sometimes physical) abuse; complete insensitivity to their cultural and religious practices; and a general lack of respect. . . . This treatment has caused many Arabs, South Asians, Muslims, and Sikhs to alter their behavior in order to avoid confrontations with authorities. Khaled Saffuri, a Lebanese man living in Great Falls, Virginia, says he makes sure to shave closely and wear a suit every time he flies; stays silent during flights and makes sure not to go to the bathroom in the middle of the flight; and sometimes avoids flying altogether in favor of long drives to his destinations in order to avoid air travel. In October 2002, Canada even issued a travel advisory warning those of its citizens born in Middle Eastern countries against traveling to the United States because of the hassles they would encounter. One celebrated Canadian, author Rohinton Mistry, who is of Indian descent and neither Arab nor Muslim, cancelled his book tour of the United States because he was "repeatedly and rudely" stopped at each airport along his tour route.

A Track Record of Failure

Recent events have demonstrated the futility of relying on profiles to predict who engages in targeted violence. In the fall of 2002, the Washington, D.C., area was shaken by a series of sniper attacks. Traditional profiles of serial killers assume that they are disaffected White men. Of course, the two men charged with the attacks are Black—an African American Gulf War Veteran, John Allen Muhammad, and Jamaican-born John Lee Malvo. Their capture was hailed by law enforcement authorities as a triumph of "old fashioned police work" and entailed the investigation of multiple leads, the pursuit of evidence nationwide, and the use of the media and the public to help develop the facts. The investigation showed how reliance on a profile "can have [police] chasing a stereotype while the real culprit slips away."

Profiling has proven to be an inaccurate indicator of other types of targeted violent crimes. Traditional profiles presumed that political assassins were male. But women—Sarah Jane Moore and Lynette "Squeaky" Fromm—carried out assassination attempts on the life of President [Gerald] Ford. And in a situation directly analogous to the one facing Arabs and Muslims today, the 10 individuals found to be spying for Japan during World War II were Caucasian. They clearly did not fit the profile that caused America to order the internment of thousands of Japanese Americans.

Old-Fashioned Methods Are Still Best

The same kind of old-fashioned police work that tracks down serial killers, assassins, and spies will help catch terrorists, not reliance on broad, inaccurate, and confusing racial stereotypes. Federal authorities have also taken many useful steps to improve airport security that pose no threat to civil rights. The use of improved technology to detect explosives, luggage matching protocols, better training of screeners, and reinforcing of cockpit doors, for example, are all prudent measures to enhance airport security. *These* are the types of weapons, along with behavior-based surveillance, that will win the war against terrorism.

Those who support the use of profiling against Arabs, South Asians, Muslims, and Sikhs argue that America must resort to profiling given the stakes. The opposite is in fact true. The stakes are so high that the nation cannot afford to use an anti-terrorism mechanism as deeply flawed as racial profiling.

5

Airlines Should Screen Passengers Who Match Terrorists' Racial Profiles

Stuart Taylor Jr.

Stuart Taylor Jr. is a senior writer and columnist for National Journal *magazine and a contributing editor for* Newsweek *magazine.*

History shows that laws permitting racial profiling are often made too hastily and prone to being abused. But even when these facts are taken into consideration, it seems clear that racial profiling should be allowed at U.S. airports. There is a much greater chance that terrorist acts will be committed by passengers of Arab descent than by others, so profiling these passengers is an important step in preventing future hijackings. This is not to say that people should be stopped solely because of their race. Rather, airport officials should be permitted to take race into account when combined with other suspicious factors. The U.S. government must make this policy crystal clear to security officials so they will understand the circumstances under which racial profiling is appropriate and acceptable.

Stuart Taylor Jr., "The Case for Using Racial Profiling at Airports," *National Journal*, September 22, 2001, pp. 2877–878. Republished with permission of *National Journal*, conveyed through Copyright Clearance Center, Inc.

With bigots harassing and violently attacking loyal Arab-Americans, it is a bit taboo in some circles to advocate racial or ethnic profiling of any kind, in any place, ever. "I'm against using race as a profiling component," even in screening would-be airline passengers, [former] Attorney General John Ashcroft declared in a September 16 [2001] television interview.

If you were boarding an airplane, wouldn't you want authorities to scrutinize Arab passengers?

Carefully Consider New Laws

At the same time, the [George W.] Bush Administration has rushed to adopt rules authorizing indefinite detention of legal immigrants, and is pressing Congress to pass immediately—with minimal scrutiny—far-reaching new powers that would (among other things) enable law enforcement officials, without presenting evidence, to lock up indefinitely foreigners suspected of terrorist links.

This, I respectfully submit, seems backwards. The new powers may be justified if they would, in fact, make us safer. But Congress should not simply assume as much without first hearing out critics who fear heavy costs to liberty with only illusory benefits to safety. The emergency measures adopted now could be with us for decades, because this emergency is not going away. So we'd better be careful. History is replete with hasty emergency legislation that we later came to regret—from the Alien and Sedition Acts [of 1798] to the [World War II–era] detention camps for Japanese-Americans—and with abuses of the new powers years later by officials whose invocations of national security proved overblown or even fraudulent.

If the Administration says it needs new powers immediately, Congress should provide that they will lapse in 30 days unless reauthorized after due deliberation.

Airline Screening Is Essential

Racial profiling of people boarding airliners, on the other hand—done politely and respectfully—may be an essential component (at least for now) of the effort to ensure that we see no more mass-murder-suicide hijackings. If you doubt this, please try a thought experiment: A few weeks hence, or a year hence, you are about to board a cross-country flight. Glancing around the departure lounge, you notice lots of white men and women; some black men and women; four young, casually dressed Latino-looking men; and three young, well-dressed Arab-looking men.

Would your next thought be, "I sure do hope that the people who let me through security without patting me down didn't violate Ashcroft's policy by frisking any of those three guys"? Or more like, "I hope somebody gave those three a good frisking to make sure they didn't have box cutters"? If the former, perhaps you care less than I do about staying alive. If the latter, you favor racial profiling—at least of Arab-looking men boarding airliners.

Airport Profiling Is a Special Case

This is not to condone the special scrutiny long given to African-Americans and other dark-skinned people in other law enforcement situations, such as when police pull them over on interstate highways in hugely disproportionate numbers and search them for drugs. Racial profiling of that kind (not to be confused with stopping and frisking young men in high-crime neighborhoods) should be deemed unconstitutional even when there is a statistically valid basis for believing that it will help catch more drug dealers or violent criminals. (There often is, given the disproportionate percentage of such crimes committed by young black men.) This benefit is far outweighed by the costs: Such racial profiling is hard to distinguish from—and sometimes involves—plain old racist harassment of groups that have long experienced discrimination at every stage of the criminal justice process. It subjects thousands of innocent people to the kind of humiliation that characterizes police states. It hurts law enforcement in the long run by fomenting fear and distrust among potential witnesses, tipsters, and jurors. It is rarely justified by any risk of imminent violence. And it makes a mockery of conservative preachings that the Constitution is colorblind.

The government has a compelling interest in preventing mass-murder-suicide hijackings, and . . . close scrutiny of Arab-looking people is narrowly tailored to protect that interest.

But stopping hijackings is different. First, preventing mass murder is infinitely more important than finding illegal drugs or guns. Second, 100 percent of the people who have hijacked airliners for the purpose of mass-murdering Americans have been Arab men. Third, a virulent perversion of Islam is the only mass movement in the world so committed to mass-murdering Americans that its fanatics are willing to kill themselves in the process. Fourth, this movement includes people who have lived legally in America for years—some of whom may be citizens—so the risk of weapons being smuggled onto airliners cannot be eliminated by giving special scrutiny only to foreign nationals.

In short, the mathematical probability that a randomly chosen Arab passenger might attempt a mass-murder-suicide hijacking—while tiny—is considerably higher than the probability that a randomly chosen white, black, Hispanic, or Asian passenger might do the same. In constitutional-law parlance, while racial profiling may be presumptively unconstitutional, that presumption is overcome in the case of airline passengers, because the government has a compelling interest in preventing mass-murder-suicide hijackings, and because close scrutiny of Arab-looking people is narrowly tailored to protect that interest.

A Clear Danger

Did Ashcroft really mean to reject any use of race "as a profiling component"? Perhaps not. In another September 16 interview, he said that people are not "suspects based solely on their race or ethnic origin." The next day, FBI Director Robert Mueller said: "We do not, have not, will not target people based solely on their ethnicity. Period."

The key word is solely. As Ashcroft and Mueller well know, the types of racial profiling that they properly deplore will rarely lead to overtly stopping or searching people based solely on their ethnicity. That's why well-dressed 60-year-old black men and women are searched for drugs a lot less than well-dressed young black men—not to mention teenagers in gangsta-rap attire.

The question is not whether Arab-looking people should be stopped, questioned, and searched based solely on their ethnicity. The question is whether airport security people should be allowed to consider ethnicity at all. The answer is yes, unless we are prepared to frisk everyone who seeks to board a plane, and until we have a security system so foolproof that we need not frisk anyone.

The Administration cannot and should not cloak its profiling policy in ambiguity.

Such a system seems attainable: It would incorporate X-ray machines as good at detecting weapons as any physical search; hi-tech equipment that can compare passengers' faces or retinas with those in government databases; impregnable doors to keep would-be hijackers from entering cockpits; rules forbidding pilots from coming out even if flight attendants' throats are being cut; and armed sky marshals. Measures like these may eventually eliminate the risk of a box cutter being used to hijack a plane. But for now, we have a clear and present danger of Arab Islamic extremists doing just that.

Clearly State the Rules

The Administration cannot and should not cloak its profiling policy in ambiguity. It is increasingly obvious that disproportionate numbers of Arabs are being interrogated, frisked, and perhaps strip-searched at airports. Unless the security people on the ground are told clearly what they should and should not do, they may engage in more (or less) racial profiling than safety requires. And if the Administration uses racial profiling while pretending to reject it, the message to police and citizens around the country will be that it's OK, as long as you lie about it. Instead, the Administration should articulate a general rule against racial profiling with one narrowly drawn exception: People who seek to board airliners will be randomly questioned and searched for potential weapons as thoroughly as, and for any reason, deemed appropriate by the responsible officials.

Arab-Americans understandably resent being singled out for special scrutiny when boarding airliners. But the alternatives . . . are worse.

Should this be the only exception? What about the dangers of terrorists smuggling bombs or guns or box cutters onto buses or trains or subways or bridges, or into tunnels or crowded stadiums or office buildings or schools or the Capitol or Disneyland?

These dangers are real. But in such settings, they are as likely to be presented by domestic terrorists such as [Oklahoma City bomber] Timothy McVeigh as by people of Arab descent. Only by crashing airliners can terrorists commit mass murder with weapons as easily concealed as box cutters and plastic knives. And only would-be mass murderers bent on suicide—the vast majority of them extremist Islamic fanatics craving martyrdom—would crash an airliner.

Airports Are a Special Danger

It's true that the gravest threats of all—biological, nuclear, and chemical terrorism—emanate mostly from Islamic extremists and do not involve airliners. But if anyone succeeded in smuggling such weapons of mass destruction across our borders, there would be so many places to hide them that racial profiling would be futile. That's why it is imperative to arrest or kill terrorists and destroy their most fearsome weapons wherever we can find them.

Arab-Americans understandably resent being singled out for special scrutiny when boarding airliners. But the alternatives—a greater risk of being killed and greater political pressure for detention of relatives and other visitors from abroad who fall under unwarranted suspicion—are worse.

6

Airlines Should Use Behavioral Profiling, Not Racial Profiling

Bruce Schneier

Bruce Schneier is an internationally known security technologist and author. His commentary on security issues appears regularly in major publications. As a noted expert, Schneier has also testified on security before the U.S. Congress on many occasions. He is the founder and chief technology officer of Counterpane Internet Security Inc., a leading protector of networked information.

In the past, U.S. customs agents have successfully identified would-be terrorists by focusing on suspicious behavior—fidgeting, sweating, and so forth. This practice is known as behavioral assessment profiling. It is entirely different from the computerized passenger profiling system now used by U.S. airlines, which depends on superficial characteristics such as race and ticket-purchase patterns. Computer profiling does not work; behavioral profiling does. Behavioral profiling can be abused if law enforcement officers start looking at physical features in addition to behavior. But as part of a carefully regulated program, it is more effective and more appropriate than racially based screening.

Bruce Schneier, "Profile: 'Hinky,'" *Boston Globe*, November 24, 2004. Reproduced by permission of the author.

On Dec. 14, 1999, Ahmed Ressam tried to enter the United States from Canada at Port Angeles, Washington. He had a suitcase bomb in the trunk of his car. A U.S. customs agent, Diana Dean, questioned him at the border. He was fidgeting, sweaty, and jittery. He avoided eye contact. In Dean's own words, he was acting "hinky." Ressam's car was eventually searched, and he was arrested.

It wasn't any one thing that tipped Dean off; it was everything encompassed in the slang term "hinky." But it worked. The reason there wasn't a bombing at Los Angeles International Airport around Christmas 1999 was because a trained, knowledgeable security person was paying attention.

Terrorists don't fit a profile and cannot be plucked out of crowds by computers.

This is "behavioral assessment" profiling. It's what customs agents do at borders all the time. It's what the Israeli police do to protect their airport and airplanes. And it's a new pilot program in the United States at Boston's Logan Airport. Behavioral profiling is dangerous because it's easy to abuse, but it's also the best thing we can do to improve the security of our air passenger system.

The Problems of Computerized Passenger Profiling

Behavioral profiling is not the same as computerized passenger profiling. The latter has been in place for years. It's a secret system, and it's a mess. Sometimes airlines decided who would undergo secondary screening, and they would choose people based on ticket purchase, frequent-flyer status, and similarity to names on government watch lists. CAPPS-2 [the second version of the Computer Assisted Passenger Pre-Screening System] was to follow, evaluating people based on government and commercial databases and assigning a "risk" score. This system was scrapped after public outcry, but another profiling system called Secure Flight will debut next year. Again, details are secret. [Secure Flight was tested in 2004–5 but ran into many problems. By mid-2006, there were no plans to implement the program.]

The problem with computerized passenger profiling is that it simply doesn't work. Terrorists don't fit a profile and cannot be plucked out of crowds by computers. Terrorists are European, Asian, African, Hispanic, and Middle Eastern, male and female, young and old. Richard Reid, the shoe bomber, was British with a Jamaican father. Jose Padilla, arrested in Chicago in 2002 as a "dirty bomb" suspect, was a Hispanic-American. Timothy McVeigh [who bombed Oklahoma City's Alfred P. Murrah Federal Building in 1995] was a white American. So was the Unabomber [convicted mail-bomb murderer Theodore "Ted" Kaczynski], who once taught mathematics at the University of California, Berkeley. The Chechens who blew up two Russian planes [in 2004] were female. Recent reports indicate that Al Qaeda is recruiting Europeans for further attacks on the United States.

Terrorists can buy plane tickets—either one way or round trip—with cash or credit cards. Mohamed Atta, the leader of the 9/11 plot, had a frequent-flyer gold card. They are a surprisingly diverse group of people, and any computer profiling system will just make it easier for those who don't meet the profile.

Behavioral assessment profiling is different. It cuts through all of those superficial profiling characteristics and centers on the person. State police are trained as screeners in order to look for suspicious conduct such as furtiveness or undue anxiety. Already at Logan Airport, the program has caught 20 people who were either in the country illegally or had outstanding warrants of one kind or another.

Objections to Behavioral Profiling

Earlier this month the ACLU [American Civil Liberties Union] of Massachusetts filed a lawsuit challenging the constitutionality of behavioral assessment profiling. The lawsuit is unlikely to succeed; the principle of "implied consent" that has been used to uphold the legality of passenger and baggage screening will almost certainly be applied in this case as well.

But the ACLU has it wrong. Behavioral assessment profiling isn't the problem. Abuse of behavioral profiling is the problem, and the ACLU has correctly identified where it can go wrong. If policemen fall back on naïve profiling by race, ethnicity, age, gender—characteristics not relevant to security—they're little better than a computer. Instead of "driving while black," the police will face accusations of harassing people for the infraction of "flying while Arab." Their actions will increase racial tensions and make them less likely to notice the real threats. And we'll all be less safe as a result.

Behavioral assessment profiling isn't a "silver bullet." It needs to be part of a layered security system, one that includes passenger baggage screening, airport employee screening, and random security checks. It's best implemented not by police but by specially trained federal officers. These officers could be deployed at airports, sports stadiums, political conventions—anywhere terrorism is a risk because the target is attractive. Done properly, this is the best thing to happen to air passenger security since reinforcing the cockpit door.

7

The Benefits of Racial Profiling Justify Some Loss of Civil Liberties

Robert A. Levy

Robert A. Levy is senior fellow in constitutional studies at the Cato Institute, a libertarian research foundation that seeks to bring policy debate to a broad public audience. A former law professor, Levy is the author of many books and newspaper articles. He is a frequent guest commentator on national radio and television programs.

The U.S. Constitution guarantees equal rights to all persons, including noncitizens. But civil rights are not absolute. The government is legally permitted to discriminate on the basis of race and/or national origin under certain conditions. Determining what these conditions should be, however, is not always easy. Three criteria should be used to decide when racial profiling is appropriate. First, using race as a factor must make a criminal profile much more effective. Second, there must be a reason to believe that many people who belong to the profiled ethnic class are guilty. Third, the benefits of profiling in any situation must exceed the costs. If these three conditions are met, the government may sacrifice some civil liberties in order to prevent future terrorist acts.

Robert A. Levy, "Ethnic Profiling: A Rational and Moral Framework," www.cato.org, October 2, 2001. Reproduced by permission.

A [2001] Gallup poll indicates that 60 percent of Americans want Arabs to undergo more intensive screening at airports. The Federal Motor Carrier Administration, which inspects trucks carrying hazardous materials, has announced that it "will be looking closely at the drivers, and if the person looks to be of Arab descent that would be enough" for stepped-up scrutiny. Those are just two instances of ethnic profiling now urged on us in the aftermath of [the] horrific events [of September 11, 2001].

But can ethnic or racial profiling ever be justified? After all, national security is a legitimate function of the federal government. Even hardcore civil libertarians concede that it would be foolish to treat civil liberties as inviolable when the lives of innocent thousands are at stake. So, what is to be done?

We should reject uncompromising views of national security.

The [U.S.] Constitution guarantees all persons, including non-citizens, due process and equal protection of the laws. Yet those rights are not absolute. The Supreme Court has insisted that the government pass a rigorous two-part test if it intends to discriminate on the basis of race or national origin. First, government must show that it has a "compelling interest" in employing its discriminatory scheme. Surely, protection against the kind of terror that we experienced on September 11 would qualify as compelling. But second, government may not discriminate unless it adopts means that are "least restrictive" when compared against alternative approaches to accomplish the same ends. That second principle will ultimately control disputes over ethnic profiling.

Drawing the Line

Where, then, should we draw the line? That's a tough question to answer. But there is an analytical framework that can be applied in determining whether ethnic profiling should be condoned. To some, that framework will seem too quantitative, even though it deals with factors that are difficult, perhaps impossible, to quantify. The goal is not to reduce the factors to a cost-benefit calculus. Rather, the goal is to frame the issues so that both practical and moral considerations can be assessed in a structured, systematic manner.

First, the easy part: At one extreme, we should reject uncompromising views of national security. Ethnic profiling cannot be defended simply by asserting that some people will be more secure. When Rep. John Cooksey (R-La.) vented his spleen—"If I see someone [who] comes in that's got a diaper on his head and a fan belt wrapped around the diaper on his head, that guy needs to be pulled over" —rational people condemned such drivel. At the other extreme, civil liberties cannot be allowed to trump national security despite overwhelming evidence that ethnic profiling could, on balance, safeguard individual rights. Imagine, for the sake of argument, that 90 percent of New Zealanders were terrorists and 90 percent of terrorists were New Zealanders. Only a fool would forbid New Zealand nationality to be added to a composite profile of suspected terrorists.

Unhappily, we are left with a vast number of tough cases that require more nuanced analysis. Toward that end, I propose the following standard, which combines two tests centering on individual rights and a third test that is explicitly utilitarian. Ethnicity may be included as one factor in a multi-factor profile if, and only if, all three of these criteria are met:

Three Criteria

First, the addition of an ethnic factor must significantly improve the effectiveness of the profile in ferreting out the guilty. Thus, if one in a hundred truck drivers who transport hazardous materials is likely to be a terrorist, and one in a hundred Arabic truck drivers who transport hazardous materials is likely to be a terrorist, the government obviously may not initiate stepped-up scrutiny because "the person looks to be of Arab descent." People who are similarly situated must be treated the same. The key, here, is evidence, not guesswork, that the profiled class is indeed different.

Second, there must be reasonable suspicion to believe that a meaningful portion of the profiled ethnic class is guilty. Otherwise, the profile will be unduly over-inclusive—vesting the sins of the guilty on the innocent. In the truck driver context, it may be that Arabs are 10 times as likely to be terrorists as non-Arabs. But if only one tenth of one percent of hazardous materials truck drivers of Arabic descent are terrorists, the addition of ethnicity to the profile cannot be justified without violating the rights of 999 out of every 1,000 persons. That seems clearly excessive to me, although I might reconsider if the government could find a way to compensate those innocent persons whose rights are abridged.

In light of recent events . . . [the government] could be asked to trade off precious civil liberties against the prospect of grievous losses . . . from terrorist acts.

Third, the benefit of including ethnicity must exceed its cost. On the benefit side, two dynamics enter into the equation: First, the chance that addition of an ethnic factor will prevent a terrorist incident that would not otherwise have been prevented. Second, a measure of the likely harm if the incident were to have occurred. The product of those two terms tells us the value of profiling ethnicity. Again, evidence rather than conjecture must control. For example, the Federal Bureau of Investigation issued an advisory warning that future terrorist attacks might come in the form of hazardous materials trucks used as rolling bombs. If substantiated, that report must certainly weigh heavily in assessing the possible damage.

On the cost side of profiling are potentially grave impositions on innocent persons, triggered by their membership in a targeted ethnic group. Naturally, a vital consideration is the scope of the imposition. We should not object if police use ethnic profiling simply to limit their investigations. Even the questioning of profiled suspects raises few concerns if the suspects are free not to answer and free to leave. But subpoenas, custodial interrogations, and extended detentions are another matter. And, of course, the number of profiled suspects is of paramount importance. It's one thing for government to stop a dozen Arab truckers of hazardous materials. It's quite different to detain all Arab non-citizens unless and until it can be proven that they pose no threat.

Civil Liberties Tradeoff is Warranted

No doubt that framework raises more questions than it answers. The devil is in the details. Still, in light of recent events, all three branches of government could be asked to trade off precious civil liberties against the prospect of grievous losses to innocent civilians from terrorist acts. That tradeoff cannot be based on seat-of-the-pants speculation, or knee-jerk invocation of theories that refuse to yield despite the exigencies of the moment. We face a new and unprecedented evil, which we must defeat without abandoning the liberties that set us apart from every other country in the world. That difficult task calls for logic, not emotion; for evidence, not rumor; and for a structured approach that weighs the competing interests rationally and morally.

8

The Benefits of Racial Profiling Cannot Justify Any Loss of Civil Liberties

Christina Fauchon

Christina Fauchon is a 2004 graduate in political science at Pace University and immediate past president of the New York Tau Chapter of Pi Gamma Mu, a national honor society recognizing excellence in the social sciences.

During World War II, the U.S. government authorized the removal of all ethnic Japanese from the nation's West Coast. In 1980, a congressional commission determined that victims of this action were owed written apologies and monetary compensation. This judgment showed that ethnic groups are prone to mistreatment during times of war and that these actions are usually regretted later. But it seems the U.S. government has failed to learn this lesson. Since the 1980s, racial profiling has been used to target possible drug offenders. And in recent years, racial profiling has been implemented in airports to protect against the terrorist threat. Not only is this practice ineffective, it is also unconstitutional. Additionally, it has severe social costs. It is the responsibility of a free, democratic country to curb this practice, which compromises people's civil rights to an unacceptable degree.

Christina Fauchon, "Counterpoint: The Case Against Profiling," *International Social Science Review*, Fall–Winter 2004, pp. 157–59. Copyright 2004 Pi Gamma Mu. Reproduced by permission.

Racial profiling can be defined as stopping and searching people passing through public areas solely because of their color, race, or ethnicity. Upon close examination of history, current events, the U.S. Constitution, case law, and both the policy itself and its social implications, one finds that racial profiling in any environment, including airports, is an unproductive and immoral policy to ensure safety.

The Japanese-American Example

Much like today, the World War II era was filled with fear and uncertainty, leading the U.S. government to incarcerate Japanese-Americans. Within three months of the Japanese attack on Pearl Harbor [on December 7, 1941], President Franklin D. Roosevelt signed Executive Order 9066 which:

> authorized the removal of all persons of Japanese descent from the west coast. Men, women and children of Japanese ancestry were falsely portrayed as a threat to national security and put into concentration camps without trial or individual review even though two thirds of them were U.S. citizens.

Today Americans are faced with a conflict between the needs of national security and the desire for freedom and personal liberty.

In 1980, Congress established the Commission on Wartime Relocation and Internment of Civilians to investigate the internment of Japanese-Americans. The commission determined that a letter of apology and $20,000 payment was owed to the victims of the government's incorrect behavior. The Japanese-American community felt vindicated—their humiliation had finally been officially acknowledged as the government accepted responsibility. The investigation and outcome showed that, in times of war, racial groups are often separated and mistreated out of fear, and that those who have mistreated them live to regret a hasty decision.

Profiling in the War on Drugs

Since the 1980s, the practice of profiling has been applied to America's war on drugs. Specifically, law-enforcement officers have detained members of minority groups in vehicles more often than whites. In conducting such stops, these officers assume that minorities commit more drug offenses, which is not the case. "In all of the published studies to date," Northeastern University law professor Deborah Ramirez points out, "minorities are no more likely to be in possession of contraband than whites. Moreover, in many of these studies, minorities, especially Latinos, are less likely to be carrying contraband." Thus, race has not proven to be a valuable or reliable resource in profiling criminals. The well-documented profiling of black people for drug offenses does nothing other than fill jail cells with black dealers and addicts while their white counterparts continue to engage in their illicit business.

Targeting behavior rather than appearance has proven to be more successful. As Ramirez reports:

> Customs revamped its stop and search procedures to remove race from the factors considered when stop decisions were made. Instead, Customs agents selected suspects for stops and searches using observational techniques and focusing on specific behaviors. . . . Customs conducted seventy percent fewer searches and their hit rates improved from approximately five percent to over fifteen percent.

If racial profiling has proven time and again not to be beneficial, it seems logical to stop using a practice that alienates an entire group of people based on their race, a factor that cannot be changed.

Identifying the Enemy

Today Americans are faced with a conflict between the needs of national security and the desire for freedom and personal liberty. We are no longer on a battlefield where the enemy is clearly recognizable. Instead, we live at a time when citizens are frightened by information that everything from apartment buildings and malls to major bridges have become military targets. This constant fear has left Americans looking for some way to identify the enemy clearly. As a consequence, the historically discredited practice of racial profiling has again been instituted in airports.

> *The United States government has a duty to protect ... the ideals upon which the nation was founded and the undeniable rights of its citizenry.*

The principles on which the United States has been built include the accepted wisdoms of freedom. The Fourteenth Amendment of the U.S. Constitution promotes two fundamental ideals to protect against racial profiling: equality and due process. The amendment states, "No state shall make or enforce any law which shall abridge the privileges or immunities of citizens of the United States; nor shall any state deprive any person of life, liberty, or property, without due process of law." To single out a group of people by race violates equal protection: The law cannot protect a group of people that is being singled out for investigation. Furthermore, profiling leaves "[a] feeling of resentment among minorities, [a] sense of hurt, and [an] increasing loss of trust in the police."

While few court cases have dealt with profiling, racial profiling is constitutionally unacceptable. Much of the justification for racial profiling is based on the notion of national security. However, in *New York Times v. United States* (1971), the U.S. Supreme Court ruled that national security cannot be placed above First Amendment rights that guarantee freedom of the press. In writing the majority opinion, Associate Justice Hugo Black declared: "The word 'security' is a broad, vague generality whose contours should not be invoked to abrogate the fundamental law embodied in the First Amendment." Accordingly, national security, because it is not clearly defined, cannot be placed above any of the fundamental rights provided for under the U.S. Constitution. In short, national security is not an acceptable excuse to deny rights by profiling. While the United States government has a duty to protect its citizens from physical harm, it also has a larger duty to protect the ideals upon which the nation was founded and the undeniable rights of its citizenry. Physical harm may come and go over time, but the rights of the people must be protected to the fullest extent at all times if such rights are to remain permanent.

Impacts of Racial Profiling

One of the most important factors to consider in arguing against racial profiling is the policy itself and the various societal impacts associated with it. It is impossible to measure the cost of alienating an entire race of people from society, and in no way can protecting the nation be used as an excuse for doing so. No benefits have been derived by targeting one race, thus making the cost of such a policy unbearable-.... While racism may exist in society, it is the duty of the government not to promote it. Yet, profiling in airports does just that! Targeting people returning from Arab countries is one thing, but targeting Arabs in general is quite another. If the doors for profiling are opened, the stage is set for future legislation that could create a police state. It is impossible to know the extent to which profiling can affect the future, but no good result can come from it.

The Western world has often been seen as racist and unfair to minorities. Racial profiling confirms these charges. As Sunera Thobani, an anti-racist scholar, points out:

> While such profiling is being lauded as "a valuable tool of law enforcement," it brings to the fore the historically problematic relationship of color to Western Democracy.

Racial profiling reveals, once again, the fundamental character of liberal democracy as a racialized project.

It is the responsibility of democracy and freedom to refute these accusations. Racial profiling is a system that has not worked and cannot work. It impacts more than how people feel; it compromises their rights. More troublesome, it can fuel genocide and other horrendous crimes that civilized, democratic nations deem repugnant and should never tolerate.

9

All Police Officers Practice Racial Profiling

Fred Reed

Writer Fred Reed has worked on staff for Army Times, *the* Washingtonian, Soldier of Fortune, Federal Computer Week, *and the* Washington Times. *His freelance opinion pieces have been published in* Playboy, Soldier of Fortune, *the* Wall Street Journal, *the* Washington Post, Harper's, *and more.*

A police officer's job is to notice consistencies of behavior. For instance, some patterns of dress and behavior consistently suggest prostitution. Others consistently suggest that a person has committed a robbery. The recognition of these patterns is a form of profiling, and it is essential to police work. The difficulty arises when a pattern applies to a racially sensitive group. This type of policing is sometimes called "racial profiling," and it is often criticized in the media. But the fact is that race and crime are very closely correlated. Law enforcement officers recognize this fact, and they act accordingly. This practice is not discrimination; it is common sense.

Lately there has been considerable honking and blowing in the press about "racial profiling" by the police. People who make their livings by being in an uproar are. Columnists emit

Fred Reed, "'Racial Profiling': The View from a Squad Car," *Fred On Everything*, 2002. Reproduced by permission of the author.

boilerplate indignation. Politicians pose. Legislators threaten to pass laws ending this iniquity. Etc. Regarding which, a few thoughts:

If columnists, and a lot of other people, spent time in police cars (I do: I've written a weekly police column for the *Washington Times* for half a decade), they would discover all manner of interesting things. For example, that "profiling" means recognition of patterns. If you call it profiling, or much better, "racial profiling," you can make it sound evil and discriminatory and establish a category of victims.

Not exactly.

To begin with, the imputation of racial hostility without establishing it is dishonest and, often, nonsensical. For example, in Washington [D.C.] the majority of cops are black, and much of the time we have had a black chief. For another, although again you have to have some first-hand knowledge of the police to know this, black cops behave just like white ones.

Cops Notice Consistencies

Cops, who are on the streets forty hours a week, notice consistencies. For example, youngish women, in fishnet stockings and plastic miniskirts up to their armpits, lounging against lampposts in red-light districts, tend to be prostitutes. So the cops check these women out. They do not check out elderly women in minks, or men with briefcases, for prostitution. The police do not have a vicious prejudice against plastic miniskirts. Nor do they hate young women. They simply know from endless experience what kinds of people are usually engaged in prostitution.

This is profiling.

They also know that scruffy homeless-looking men, walking down back alleys in pricey residential neighborhoods with VCRs under their arms, are quite likely to have stolen the VCRs. So they check them out.

This too is profiling.

Possibly a woman in a Saran-wrap tank top and a thong bikini just likes Saran wrap. Maybe she's wearing a thong bikini because the weather is warm. Maybe she is on her way to a costume party. Or took a wrong turn on the way to the beach. And perhaps the scruffy guy is an eccentric millionaire. . ., taking his VCR for a walk. Maybe some charitable rich guy gave a bum a VCR out of the kindness of his heart.

So, yes, you could say that checking out half-naked women on street corners, or derelicts with expensive items, is discrimination. They might be innocent, yes. And it's certainly profiling.

The fact is that most street-level drug dealers in Washington are black. . . . So cops check them out.

But it is the soul of police work. Scruffy people who go into expensive department stores, in baggy clothes, and then proceed to look furtively around them and brush up against merchandise, are often shoplifters. This recognition is profiling. Perhaps they are innocent—honest paranoids, or have merchandise-brushing personality disorder. But people who work in security in those stores know what shoplifters look like. And so they watch them.

Security personnel at airports look for certain kinds of people—those who fit the terrorist profile. IRS audits people who meet certain standards. On and on. It isn't that airports carry irrational prejudices against people who twitch and sweat and have ticking shoulder bags (or whatever is on the profile: I don't know). If you wanted to sit home and twitch, or if they knew for a fact that the ticking came from an innocent alarm clock, they would have nothing against you whatever. But they know from experience that certain things give away terrorists. So they check out those people. Do you want them to stop?

Race-Based Profiling

Problems arise when the targeted class belongs to a politically sensitive group, especially if it is a racial group other than white. (Although profiling can affect whites. If the police check out a slinky white woman who keeps approaching men in the bar of a classy hotel, she may turn out to be a promiscuous heiress, which it isn't illegal to be. She raises Cain because she has been humiliated. And she probably has been.)

Cops deal in facts, not theories. Cops check out those who fit the patterns.

What usually makes the news is profiling of blacks. The fact is that most street-level drug dealers in Washington are black. Blacks are heavily involved in transportation of drugs for sale. Should you doubt this, ask any cop of any color. Dealers look and behave in certain ways, and are certain kinds of people. They are black, scruffy, young, hang in certain places, display certain body language when cops are around. So cops check them out.

The downside of profiling is that, while young black males on I-95, wearing scruffy clothes and driving rentals with no baggage, are in fact often drug couriers, often they aren't. Sometimes they are innocent kids of black doctors, wearing scruffy clothes because it is the current teenage way of annoying their elders. These kids get very sick, very fast, of constantly being stopped and humiliated in front of their girlfriends. I don't blame them. Your choice: Let the drugs through to avoid embarrassing the innocent kid, or embarrass the kid and get the drugs. That is precisely the choice. Let's not pretend otherwise.

It is also true, but verboten to point out, that race and crime are very closely correlated. When I go into the security rooms of the big department stores around the Pentagon (usually to pick up a shoplifter), the photographs of previously collared boosters are almost entirely black. The region isn't. Now, you can explain this correspondence as you like: You can blame society, blacks, whites, capitalists, racists, the weather. You can say it's my fault, your fault, God's fault. But it's a fact, politically palatable or not. Cops deal in facts, not theories.

Cops check out those who fit the patterns.

Racial Profiling Is Not Discrimination

Racial discrimination? Seldom. The same majority-black cops who check out likely black drug dealers would just as quickly check out whites if the whites fit a pattern. They assuredly do check out prosperous-looking whites with Virginia and Maryland tags who park in bad black sections of Washington. Anti-white prejudice? Nope. They know they are there, almost certainly, to buy drugs. Whites from McLean don't have poor black friends in [Washington, D.C., neighborhood] Anacostia.

10

Racial Profiling in Law Enforcement Is a Myth

Heather Mac Donald

Heather Mac Donald is a nonpracticing lawyer and a fellow at the Manhattan Institute, a conservative think tank. She is an editor and regular contributor to urban affairs magazine City Journal *and has written for many other national publications. Her latest book,* Are Cops Racist?, *investigates the controversy over racial profiling in American law enforcement.*

Traditionally, anti–racial profiling crusaders have claimed that police stop too many minorities for traffic violations and other minor infractions. This behavior has been described as racist. A landmark study on traffic patterns on the New Jersey Turnpike, however, finds that black drivers actually do drive more recklessly than white drivers. This study proves that police are not racists; rather, they are just doing their jobs. But although the New Jersey study was well designed and statistically sound, the U.S. Department of Justice tried to block its release because its conclusions were unpopular. Politics should not be allowed to interfere with facts. Acknowledging that racial profiling does not occur systematically in law enforcement will dramatically improve relationships between police and the communities they serve.

The anti-racial profiling juggernaut has finally met its nemesis: the truth. According to a new study, black drivers on the New Jersey Turnpike are twice as likely to speed as white drivers, and are even more dominant among drivers breaking 90 miles per hour. This finding demolishes the myth of racial profiling. Precisely for that reason, the [George W.] Bush Justice Department tried to bury the report so the profiling juggernaut could continue its destructive campaign against law enforcement. What happens next will show whether the politics of racial victimization now trump all other national concerns.

Establishing Violator Benchmarks

Until now, the anti-police crusade that travels under the banner of "ending racial profiling" has traded on ignorance. Its spokesmen went around the country charging that the police were stopping "too many" minorities for traffic infractions or more serious violations. The reason, explained the anti-cop crowd, was that the police were racist.

They can argue that no more. The new turnpike study, commissioned by the New Jersey attorney general, solves one of the most vexing problems in racial profiling analysis: establishing a violator benchmark. To show that the police are stopping "too many" members of a group, you need to know, at a minimum, the rate of lawbreaking among that group—the so-called violator benchmark. Only if the rate of stops or arrests greatly exceeds the rate of criminal behavior should our suspicions be raised. But most of the studies that the ACLU [American Civil Liberties Union] and defense attorneys have proffered to show biased behavior by the police only used crude population measures as the benchmark for comparing police activity—arguing, say, that if 24 percent of speeding stops on a particular stretch of highway were of black drivers, in a city or state where blacks make up 19 percent of the population, the police are over-stopping blacks.

Such an analysis is clearly specious, since it fails to say what percentage of *speeders* are black, but the data required to rebut it were not available. Matthew Zingraff, a criminologist at North Carolina State University, explains why: "Everybody was terrified. Good statisticians were throwing up their hands and saying, 'This is one battle you'll never win. I don't want to be called a racist.'" Even to suggest studying the driving behavior of different racial groups was to demonstrate one's bigotry, as Zingraff himself discovered when he proposed such research in North Carolina and promptly came under attack. Such investigations violate the reigning fiction in anti-racial profiling rhetoric: that all groups commit crime and other infractions at equal rates. It follows from this central fiction that any differences in the rate at which the police interact with certain citizens result only from police bias, not from differences in citizen behavior.

Jumping on the Anti-Profiling Bandwagon

Despite the glaring flaws in every racial profiling study heretofore available, the press and the politicians jumped on the anti-profiling bandwagon. How could they lose? They showed their racial sensitivity, and, as for defaming the police without evidence, well, you don't have to worry that the *New York Times* will be on your case if you do.

No institution made more destructive use of racial profiling junk science than the [Bill] Clinton Justice Department. Armed with the shoddy studies, it slapped costly consent decrees on police departments across the country, requiring them to monitor their officers' every interaction with minorities, among other managerial intrusions.

No consent decree was more precious to the anti-police agenda than the one slapped on New Jersey. In 1999, then-governor Christine Todd Whitman had declared her state's highway troopers guilty of racial profiling, based on a study of consent searches that would earn an F in a freshmen statistics class. (In a highway consent search, an officer asks a driver for permission to search his car, usually for drugs or weapons.) The study, executed by the New Jersey attorney general, lacked crucial swaths of data on stops, searches, and arrests, and compensated for the lack by mixing data from wildly different time periods. Most fatally, the attorney general's study lacked any benchmark of the rate at which different racial groups transport illegal drugs on the turnpike. Its conclusion that the New Jersey state troopers were searching "too many" blacks for drugs was therefore meaningless.

Hey, no problem! exclaimed the Clinton Justice Department. *Here's your consent decree and high-priced federal monitor; we'll expect a lengthy report every three months on your progress in combating your officers' bigotry.*

Universally decried as racists, New Jersey's troopers started shunning discretionary law-enforcement activity. Consent searches on the turnpike, which totaled 440 in 1999, the year that the anti-racial profiling campaign got in full swing, dropped to an astoundingly low 11 in the six months that ended October 31, 2001. At the height of the drug war in 1988, the troopers filed 7,400 drug charges from the turnpike, most of those from consent searches; in 2000, they filed 370 drug charges, a number that doubtless has been steadily dropping since then. It is unlikely that drug trafficking has dropped on New Jersey's main highway by anything like these percentages.

"There's a tremendous demoralizing effect of being guilty until proven innocent," explains trooper union vice president Dave Jones. "Anyone you interact with can claim you've made a race-based stop, and you spend years defending yourself." Arrests by state troopers have also been plummeting since the Whitman–Justice Department racial profiling declaration. Not surprisingly, murder jumped 65 percent in Newark, a major destination of drug traffickers, between 2000 and 2001. In an eerie replay of the eighties' drug battles, Camden is considering inviting the state police back to fight its homicidal drug gangs.

Race Has Nothing to Do with It

But one thing did not change after the much-publicized consent decree: the proportion of blacks stopped on the turnpike for speeding continued to exceed their proportion in the driving population. *Man, those troopers must be either really dumb or really racist!* thought most observers, including the New Jersey attorney general, who accused the troopers of persistent profiling.

It turns out that the police stop blacks more for speeding because they speed more. Race has nothing to do with it.

Faced with constant calumny for their stop rates, the New Jersey troopers asked the attorney general to do the unthinkable: study speeding behavior on the turnpike. If it turned out that all groups drive the same, as the reigning racial profiling myths hold, then the troopers would accept the consequences.

Well, we now know that the troopers were neither dumb nor racist; they were merely doing their jobs. According to the study commissioned by the New Jersey attorney general and leaked first to the *New York Times* and then to the Web, blacks make up 16 percent of the drivers on the turnpike, and 25 percent of the speeders in the 65-mile-per-hour zones, where profiling complaints are most common. (The study counted only those going more than 15 miles per hour over the speed limit as speeders.) Black drivers speed twice as much as white drivers, and speed at reckless levels even more. Blacks are actually stopped less than their speeding behavior would predict—they are 23 percent of those stopped.

The devastation wrought by this study to the anti-police agenda is catastrophic. The medieval Vatican could not have been more threatened had [17th-century physicist, astronomer, and philosopher] Galileo offered photographic proof of the solar system. It turns out that the police stop blacks more for speeding because they speed more. Race has nothing to do with it.

This is not a politically acceptable result. And the researchers who conducted the study knew it. Anticipating a huge backlash should they go public with their findings, they checked and rechecked their data. But the results always came out the same.

Government Opposition

Being scientists, not politicians, they prepared to publish their study this past January, come what may. *Not so fast!* commanded the now-Bush Department of Justice [DOJ]. *We have a few questions for you.* And the Bush DOJ, manned by the same attorneys who had so eagerly snapped up the laughable New Jersey racial profiling report in 1999, proceeded to pelt the speeding researchers with a series of increasingly desperate objections.

The elegant study, designed by the Public Service Research Institute in Maryland, had taken photos with high-speed camera equipment and a radar gun of nearly 40,000 drivers on the turnpike. The researchers then showed the photos to a team of three evaluators, who identified the race of the driver. The evaluators had no idea if the drivers in the photos had been speeding. The photos were then correlated with speeds.

The driver identifications are not reliable! whined the Justice Department. The researchers had established a driver's race by agreement among two of the three evaluators. So in response to DOJ's complaint, the researchers reran their analysis, using only photos about which the evaluators had reached unanimous agreement. The speeding ratios came out identically as before.

The data are incomplete! shouted the Justice Department next. About one third of the photos had been unreadable, because of windshield glare that interfered with the camera, or the driver's position. *Aha!* said the federal attorneys. *Those unused photos would change your results!* But that is a strained argument. The only way that the 12,000 or so unreadable photos would change the study's results would be if windshield glare or a seating position that obstructed the camera disproportionately affected one racial group. Clearly, they do not.

Nevertheless, DOJ tried to block the release of the report until its objections were answered. "Based on the questions we have identified, it may well be that the results reported in the draft report are wrong or unreliable," portentously wrote Mark Posner, a Justice lawyer held over from the Clinton era.

DOJ's newfound zeal for pseudo-scientific nitpicking is remarkable, given its laissez-faire attitude toward earlier slovenly reports that purported to show racial profiling. Where it gets its new social-science expertise is also a mystery, since according to North Carolina criminologist Matthew Zingraff, "there's not a DOJ attorney who knows a thing about statistical methods and analysis." Equally surprising is Justice's sudden unhappiness with the Public Service Research Institute, since it approved the selection of the institute for an earlier demographic study of the turnpike.

The institute proposed a solution to the impasse: Let us submit the study to a peer-reviewed journal or a neutral body like the National Academy of Sciences. If a panel of our scientific peers determines the research to be sound, release the study then. *No go,* said the Justice Department. *That study ain't seeing the light of day.*

Robert Voas, the study's co-author, is amazed by Justice's intransigence. "I think it's very unfortunate that the politics have gotten in the way of science," he says, choosing his words carefully. "The scientific system has not been allowed to move as it should have in this situation."

While racist cops undoubtedly do exist, . . . the evidence shows that systematic racial profiling by police does not exist.

Systematic Racial Profiling Does Not Exist

As DOJ and the New Jersey attorney general stalled, *The Record* of Bergen posted the report on the Web, forcing the state attorney general to release it officially. Now the damage control begins in earnest. Everyone with a stake in the racial profiling myth, from the state attorney general to the ACLU [American Civil Liberties Union] to defense attorneys who have been getting drug dealers out of jail and back on the streets by charging police racism, is trying to minimize the significance of the findings. But they are fighting a rear-guard battle. Waiting in the wings are other racial profiling studies by statisticians who actually understand the benchmark problem: Matthew Zingraff's pioneering traffic research in North Carolina, due out in April [2002], as well as sound studies in Pennsylvania, New York, and Miami. Expect many of the results to support the turnpike data, since circumstantial evidence from traffic fatalities and drunk-driving tests have long suggested different driving behaviors among different racial groups. While racist cops undoubtedly do exist, and undoubtedly they are responsible for isolated instances of racial profiling, the evidence shows that systematic racial profiling by police does not exist.

The Bush administration, however desperate to earn racial sensitivity points, should realize that far more than politics is at stake in the poisonous anti-racial profiling agenda. It has strained police-community relations and made it more difficult for the police to protect law-abiding citizens in inner-city neighborhoods. The sooner the truth about policing gets out, the more lives will be saved, and the more communities will be allowed to flourish freed from the yoke of crime.

11

Racial Profiling Is Useful if Properly Regulated

Peter H. Schuck

Peter H. Schuck has been a professor at Yale Law School since 1981. He is the author of many articles and books, many of which address civil rights issues.

The job of counterterrorism screening in post-9/11 America is huge and incredibly difficult for security officers. The only practical way to figure out which people are potentially more dangerous than others is by using stereotypes—assumptions that link a person's observable qualities to possible behaviors. Stereotypes—a form of racial profiling—are a useful antiterrorism tool because they are usually right. Of course, stereotypes are sometimes wrong as well, and using them can offend people. For this reason, the use of stereotypes must be carefully thought out and enforced. Yet racial profiling is inevitable in the aftermath of the terrorist attacks of September 11, 2001.

The furor about racial profiling is easy to understand. "Driving while black" and "flying while Arab" are emblems of the indignities that law enforcement officials are said to inflict on minorities on the basis of demeaning stereotypes

Peter H. Schuck, "A Case for Profiling," *In Meditations of a Militant Moderate: Cool Views on Hot Topics*. Rowman & Littlefield, 2006. Reproduced by permission of the author.

and racial prejudice. This is no laughing matter. Respect for the rule of law means that people must not be singled out for enforcement scrutiny simply because of their race or ethnicity.

Or does it? Much turns on the meaning of "simply" in the last sentence. Profiling is not only inevitable but sensible public policy under certain conditions and with appropriate safeguards against abuse. After September 11, the stakes in deciding when and how profiling may be used and how to remedy abuses when they occur could not be higher.

A Debate About Values

A fruitful debate on profiling properly begins with our values as a society. The most important of these, of course, is self-defense, without which no other values can be realized. But we should be wary of claims that we must sacrifice our ideals in the name of national security; this means that other ideals remain central to the inquiry. The one most threatened by profiling is the principle that all individuals are equal before the law by reason of their membership in a political community committed to formal equality. In most but not all respects, we extend the same entitlement to aliens who are present in the polity legally or illegally. Differential treatment must meet a burden of justification in the case of racial classifications, a very high one.

This ideal has a corollary: Government may not treat individuals arbitrarily. To put this principle another way, it must base its action on information that is reliable enough to justify its exercise of power over free individuals. How good must the information be? The law's answer is that it depends. Criminal punishment requires proof beyond a reasonable doubt, while a tort judgment demands only the preponderance of the evidence. Health agencies can often act with little more than a rational suspicion that a substance might be dangerous. A consular official can deny a visa if in her "opinion" the applicant is likely to become a public charge and unlike the previous examples, courts may not review this decision. Information good enough for one kind of decision, then, is not nearly good enough for others. Context is everything.

Screening Is Difficult

This brings us to profiling by law enforcement officials. Consider the context in which an FBI agent must search for the September 11 terrorists, or a security officer at a railroad and airline terminal must screen for new ones. Vast numbers of individuals pass through the officer's line of vision, and they do so only fleetingly, for a few seconds at most. As a result, the official must make a decision about each of them within those few seconds, unless she is prepared to hold all of them up for the time it will take to interrogate each, one by one. She knows absolutely nothing about these individuals, other than the physical characteristics that she can immediately observe, and learning more about them through interrogation will take a lot of time. The time this would take is costly to her task; each question she stops to ask will either allow others to pass by unnoticed or prolong the wait of those in the already long, steadily lengthening line. The time is even more costly to those waiting in line; for them, more than for her, time is money and opportunity. Politicians know how their constituents hate lines and constantly press her along with customs, immigration, and toll officials to shorten them.

At the same time, her risks of being wrong are dramatically asymmetrical. If she stops everyone, she will cause all of the problems just described and all of the people (except one, perhaps) will turn out to be perfectly innocent. On the other hand, if she fails to stop the one person among them who is in fact a terrorist, she causes a social calamity of incalculable proportions. In choosing, as she must, between these competing risks, her self-interest and the social interest will drive her in the direction of avoiding calamity. The fact that society also tells her to be evenhanded only adds to her dilemma, while providing no useful guidance as to what to do, given these incentives.

Stereotypes Are a Useful Tool

So what should she do? We can get at this question by asking what we would do were we in her place. To answer this question, we need not engage in moral speculation but can look to our own daily experiences. Each day, we all face choices that are very similar in structure, albeit far less consequential. We must make decisions very rapidly about things that matter to us. We know that our information is inadequate to the choice, but we also know that we cannot in the time available get information that is sufficiently better to improve our decision significantly. We consider our risks of error, which are often asymmetrical. Because we must momentarily integrate all this uncertainty into a concrete choice, we resort to shortcuts to decisionmaking. . . .

Although all stereotypes are overbroad, most are probably correct much more often than they are wrong.

The most important and universal of these tactical shortcuts is the stereotype. The advantage of stereotypes is that they economize on information, enabling us to choose quickly when our information is inadequate. This is a great, indeed indispensable virtue, precisely because this problem is ubiquitous in daily life, so ubiquitous that we scarcely notice it; nor do we notice how often we use stereotypes to solve it. Indeed, we could not live without stereotypes. We use them in order to predict how others will behave as when we assume that blacks will vote Democratic (though many do not) and to anticipate others' desires, needs, or expectations, as when we offer help to disabled people (though some of them find this presumptuous). We use them when we take safety precautions when a large, unkempt, angry-looking man approaches us on a dark street (though he may simply be asking directions), and when we assume that higher-status schools are better (though they often prove to be unsuitable). Such assumptions are especially important in a mass society where people know less and less about one another.

The Downside of Stereotypes

Stereotypes, of course, have an obvious downside: They are sometimes wrong, almost by definition. After all, if they were wrong all the time, no rational person would use them, and if they were never wrong, they would be indisputable facts, not stereotypes. Stereotypes fall somewhere in between these extremes, but it is hard to know precisely where, because we seldom know precisely how accurate they are. Although all stereotypes are overbroad, most are probably correct much more often than they are wrong; that is why they are useful. But when a stereotype is wrong, those who are exceptions to it naturally feel that they have not been treated equally as individuals, and they are right. Their uniqueness is being overlooked so that others can use stereotypes for the much larger universe of cases where the stereotypes are true and valuable. In this way, the palpable claims of discrete individuals are sacrificed to a disembodied social interest. This sacrifice offends not just them but others among us who identify with their sense of injustice, and when their indignation is compounded by the discourtesy or bias of bag checkers or law enforcement agents, the wound is even more deeply felt.

Stereotypes and the Law

This is where the law comes in. When we view these stereotype-based injustices as sufficiently grave, we prohibit them. Even then, however, we do so only in a qualified way that expresses our ambivalence. Civil rights law, for example, proscribes racial, gender, disability, and age stereotyping. At the same time, it allows government, employers, and others to adduce a public interest or business reason strong enough to justify using them. The law allows religious groups to hire only coreligionists. Officials drawing legislative districts may to some extent treat all members of a minority group as if they all had the same political interests. The military can bar women from certain combat roles. Employers can assume that women are usually less suitable for jobs requiring very heavy lifting. Such practices reflect stereotypes that are thought to be reasonable in general, though false as to particular individuals.

Can the same be said of racial or ethnic profiling? Again, context is everything. . . . No one would think it unjust for our officer to screen for Osama bin Laden, who is a very tall man with a beard and turban, by stopping all men meeting that general description. This is so not only because the stakes in apprehending him are immense but also because in making instantaneous decisions about whom to stop, the official can use gender, size, physiognomy, and dress as valuable clues. She would be irresponsible and incompetent not to do so even though every man she stopped was likely to be a false positive and thus to feel unjustly treated for having been singled out.

Racial profiling in more typical law enforcement settings can raise difficult moral questions. Suppose that society views drug dealing as a serious vice, and that a disproportionate number of drug dealers are black men although of course many are not. Would this stereotype justify stopping black men simply because of their color? Clearly not. The law properly requires more particularized evidence of wrongdoing. Suppose further, however, that police were to observe a black man engaging in the ostensibly furtive behavior that characterizes most but not all drug dealers' behavior also engaged in by some innocent men. Here, the behavioral stereotype would legally justify stopping the man. But what if the officer relied on both stereotypes in some impossible-toparse combination? What if the behavioral stereotype alone had produced a very close call, and the racial one pushed it over the line?

Crafting a Sensible Policy

Although I cannot answer all these questions, most critics of racial profiling do not even ask them. A wise policy will insist that the justice of profiling depends on a number of variables. How serious is the crime risk? How do we feel about the relative costs of false positives and false negatives? How accurate is the stereotype? How practicable is it to pursue the facts through an individualized inquiry rather than through stereotypes? If stereotypes must be used, are there some that rely on less incendiary and objectionable factors?

A sensible profiling policy will also recognize that safeguards become more essential as the enforcement process progresses. Stereotypes that are reasonable at the stage of deciding whom to screen for questioning may be unacceptable at the later stages of arrest and prosecution, when official decisions should be based on more individualized information and when lawyers and other procedural safeguards can be made available. Screening officials can be taught about the many exceptions to even serviceable stereotypes, to recognize them when they appear, and to behave in ways that encourage those being screened not to take it personally.

It is now a cliché that September 11 changed our world. Profiling is bound to be part of the new dispensation. Clearer thinking and greater sensitivity to its potential uses and abuses can help produce both a safer and a more just America.

12

U.S. Racial Profiling Policies Are Based on Political Correctness, Not Logic

Michelle Malkin

Conservative commentator Michelle Malkin is best known for her nationally syndicated newspaper column, which appears in nearly two hundred newspapers across America. Malkin is also a book author, a FOX News Channel contributor, and a former editorial writer and columnist for the Seattle Times *and the* Los Angeles Daily News.

Religious profiling is an essential tool in a war where the enemies are religious extremists. Yet antiprofiling advocates loudly proclaim that any *use of racial profiling is motivated by blind prejudice. As a result of this attitude, agents within the Federal Bureau of Investigation are now afraid to take any action that might be criticized as discriminatory. In retrospect, however, it appears that such action could have prevented the 9/11 attacks. If the government wishes to be effective in the war on terror, it must ignore the media's criticism and use racial profiling whenever and wherever it is warranted.*

Michelle Malkin, *In Defense of Internment: The Case for "Racial Profiling" in World War II and the War on Terror*, Washington, DC: Regnery, 2004. Copyright © 2004 Henry Regnery Company. All rights reserved. Reprinted by special permission of Regnery Publishing Inc., Washington D.C.

Fear of a political backlash has caused President [George W.] Bush, [former] Attorney General John Ashcroft, [former] Homeland Security chief Tom Ridge, and the Pentagon to publicly disavow threat profiling. Consider the reaction of Sarah Eltantawi, communications director of the Muslim Public Affairs Council, to the idea that the twelve Muslim chaplains currently serving in the armed forces should be vetted more carefully than military rabbis or priests. When asked about this in a FOX News interview, Eltantawi brought up—you guessed it—Japanese internment. Never mind that the Muslim chaplains were trained by a radical Wahhabi school and certified by a Muslim group founded by Abdurahman Alamoudi, charged in September 2003 with accepting hundreds of thousands of dollars from Libya, a U.S.-designated sponsor of terrorism. Bowing to Eltantawi and her allies, the Pentagon pressed forward with a review of all two thousand eight hundred military chaplains, rather than focusing exclusively on the twelve Muslim chaplains. The refusal to be discriminating was, as Senator Jon Kyl (a Republican from Arizona) acknowledged, the "height of politically correct stupidity."

Religious Profiling

The same fear of a PC backlash has hampered effective Federal Bureau of Investigation (FBI) counterterrorism efforts. When the FBI announced plans to tally the number of mosques in the country—a basic intelligence-gathering building block—Muslim civil rights groups and their supporters balked. It is an act of "political repression" by the U.S. government, said the American Muslim Council. "It is religious profiling of the worst kind and must be rescinded if America is to maintain respect for religious freedom and for equal justice under the law," complained CAIR [Council on American-Islamic Relations] Executive Director Nihad Awad.

It is indeed religious profiling, and it is an essential tool in a war where the enemies are religious extremists carrying out a religious crusade to kill Americans. If a Catholic, Protestant, Jewish, or Hindu sect declared the equivalent of jihad on America and killed thousands of Americans, the FBI would be thoroughly justified—indeed, obligated—to gather basic intelligence data on churches, congregations, or temples. Manhattan Institute scholar Heather Mac Donald, who has written cogently on racial profiling and national security before and after the September 11 attacks, observed, "Looking for Muslims for participation in Muslim jihad is not playing the odds, it is following an ironclad tautology. Nevertheless, anti-police and Arab advocates have co-opted the discourse about racial profiling to tar all rational law-enforcement efforts against Islamic terrorism as an outgrowth of blind prejudice."

When we are under attack, "racial profiling"—or more precisely, threat profiling—is justified.

A Culture of Fear

The hypocritical opponents of FBI profiling damn agents as bigots when they attempt the most modest of surveillance measures based on race, religion, or other politically incorrect criteria—then damn them as bumblers when they fail to act on information gathered through those means. In the summer of 2001, Phoenix FBI agent Kenneth Williams urged his superiors to investigate militant Muslim men whom he suspected of training in U.S. flight schools as part of al Qaeda missions. He had become suspicious of Arab students enrolled at an Arizona aviation academy. Williams's recommendation to canvass flight schools was rejected, FBI director Robert Mueller later admitted, partly because at least one agency official raised concerns that the plan could be viewed as discriminatory racial profiling. "If we went out and started canvassing, we'd get in trouble for targeting Arab Americans," one FBI official told the *Los Angeles Times*. Several law enforcement officials told the paper that "a culture of fear" had pervaded FBI counter-terrorism agents. Mueller acknowledged that if Williams's Phoenix profiling memo had been shared with the agency's Minneapolis office, which had unsuccessfully sought a special intelligence warrant to search suspected twentieth hijacker Zacarias Moussaoui's laptop computer, the warrant might have been granted. And 9/11 might still be nothing more than a phone number.

The *New York Times* characterized the FBI's failure to take Williams's advice as "one indicator of the paralytic fear of risk-taking" at the bureau. But is there any doubt that the *Times* would have been the first to whip out its broad brush and pot of racist-smearing tar if it had caught wind of Williams's memo *before* September 11? Maureen Dowd, the *Times*'s resident chaise lounge general, jumped all over Mueller's admission: "Now we know the truth: The 9/11 terrorists could have been stopped if . . . the law enforcement agencies had not been so inept, obstructionist, arrogant, antiquated, bloated and turf-conscious—and timid about racial profiling."

Where exactly does Dowd think such timidity stems from? Her colleague Nicholas Kristof was honest enough to acknowledge the mau-mauing media's role in a piece titled "Liberal Reality Check":

> As we gather around FBI headquarters sharpening our machetes and watching the buzzards circle overhead, let's be frank: There's a whiff of hypocrisy in the air. One reason aggressive agents were restrained as they tried to go after Zacarias Moussaoui is that liberals like myself—and the news media caldron in which I toil and trouble—have regularly excoriated law enforcement authorities for taking shortcuts and engaging in racial profiling. As long as we're pointing fingers, we should peer into the mirror. The timidity of

bureau headquarters is indefensible. But it reflected not just myopic careerism but also an environment (that we who care about civil liberties helped create) in which officials were afraid of being assailed as insensitive storm troopers.

Desperate Times, Disparate Measures

In war, desperate times sometimes call for disparate measures. Make no mistake: I am not advocating rounding up all Arabs or Muslims and tossing them into camps, but when we are under attack, "racial profiling"—or more precisely, threat profiling—is justified. It is unfortunate that well-intentioned Arabs and Muslims might be burdened because of terrorists who share their race, nationality, or religion. But any inconvenience, no matter how bothersome or offensive, is preferable to being incinerated at your office desk by a flaming hijacked plane.

13

Racial Profiling Has a Heavy Social Cost

Amnesty International

Amnesty International is a worldwide human rights activist movement with more than 1.8 million members in more than 150 countries and territories. The organization does research and takes action designed to end abuses of people's rights to physical and mental integrity, freedom of conscience and expression, and freedom from discrimination.

The practice of racial profiling has three primary social costs: It upsets individuals, it causes entire communities to distrust law enforcement officers, and it makes domestic security less effective. Although the first two effects are easy to understand, it is sometimes harder for people to accept that racial profiling is bad for national security. But many examples show that race-based law enforcement practices distract officers and make it harder for them to perceive real threats. U.S. strategies for fighting terrorism at home do not take these past examples into account. It is likely that this failure will have a continuing negative impact on American society and safety.

Amnesty International "Threat and Humiliation: Racial Profiling, Domestic Security, and Human Rights in the United States," www.amnestyusa.org, September 2004. Reproduced by permission.

Protecting individuals' human rights is about respecting the ideals of universal human freedom and dignity. It is also about creating and maintaining an environment in which good government, including effective law enforcement, is possible. Thus, when analyzing the cost of any human rights abuse, it is not only important to explore its impact on the affected individual, but also its effect on their community and the nation as a whole.

The social costs of racial profiling ultimately affect entire communities.

The social cost of racial profiling can be generally grouped into three broad categories:

- distressed individuals

- disconnected communities

- diminished domestic security capabilities

Distressed Individuals

As many of the cases reported to AIUSA [Amnesty International USA] illustrate, there is a significant amount of empirical data suggesting a strong correlation between racial profiling and excessive use of force. However, even when excessive force is not involved, incidents of racial profiling often have a long-lasting impact on their victims. Individuals who reported such incidents to AIUSA during the last 12 months frequently cited:

- feelings of humiliation, depression, helplessness, anger, and fear

- diminished trust in law enforcement

- reluctance to turn to law enforcement for help

People who witnessed such incidents, especially those that involved excessive force, frequently said they had been affected in similar ways. One man, whose young daughter witnessed him being pepper sprayed by a police officer during a profiling incident, said that she now frequently cries when she sees a police officer.

Disenfranchised Communities

Indeed, the social costs of racial profiling ultimately affect entire communities. The community-level costs of racial profiling include:

Fear and mistrust of police, leading to a lack of cooperation with officers and a reluctance to report crimes. Example: In New York City, Monami Maulik of Desi Rising Up and Moving (DRUM) discussed the widespread fear among affected communities. In particular, after the attacks of 9/11, Ms. Maulik says that Arab, Muslim, South Asian, and Middle-Eastern youth stopped by police are often asked about their country of origin and immigration status. This has reportedly produced widespread fear within these communities. She says, "[There is fear] . . . not just about detention or deportation for people affected by that, but to do simple things like going to the emergency room or calling 911 or calling the fire department. . . . "

Alienation of minority communities from police. Example: Dr. Jesse Ghannam, President of the San Francisco American-Arab Anti-Discrimination Committee (ADC-SF) testified, ". . . the community that I speak to every day is so fearful right now when they see the badge, when they see the blue uniform. . . . [S]o when you're asking me, is there room for any dialogue . . . with the law enforcement community, I'd have to say the time is not right."

Reinforcement of segregation of minority communities. Example: Florentina Rendo of Hope Fair Housing Center highlighted the city of West Chicago's recent passage of restrictive housing ordinances. Once passed, these ordinances are reportedly carried out in a discriminatory fashion against Latino immigrants with the help of the police. She said, "That's just another way of trying to keep away minorities from western suburbs."

Racial profiling directly threatens the security of the nation as a whole.

Emotional and psychological distress for victims. Example: John Burris, a nationally known civil rights attorney and author, testified about the impact of racial profiling on victims. He says, "... the pain was as great for those people who had been beaten as it was for those who had been stopped [based on race]...."

Poor police performance. Example: According to Captain Ron Davis of the Oakland Police Department, racial profiling is "... one of the most ineffective strategies, and I call it nothing less than lazy, sloppy police work." Because all communities depend upon the police for their safety and security, any police strategy that undermines their performance undermines the quality of life for local residents.

Disproportionate incarceration of racial and ethnic minorities. The disproportionately large increase in incarceration rates for African Americans and Latinos has been tied to the use of racial profiling in the "War on Drugs." In one instance, in the small town of Tulia, Texas, nearly 10 percent of the African-American population was arrested and convicted on trumped up drug charges in 1999, with sentences "ranging up to 341 years." In 2003, the court found that the convictions were secured based solely on the testimony of a corrupt police officer with a shady history of police work and the defendants were subsequently released. ...

It is easy for many Americans to understand how racial profiling may negatively impact targeted individuals, their communities, and the relationship between those communities and the police. Similarly, many can see that when communities become estranged from their police forces, it becomes easier for crime to go unreported in those communities and criminal activity to flourish in ways that may ultimately harm the quality of life for neighboring communities as well. What is often harder for people to appreciate is the way in which racial profiling directly threatens the security of the nation as a whole.

Domestic Security Impact of Over-Generalized Suspicion

Racial profiling is a liability in the effort to make our nation safer. Race-based policing practices have frequently distracted law enforcement officials and made them blind to dangerous behaviors and real threats. Moreover, this is a lesson that law enforcement should have internalized a long time ago. To help illustrate the grave cost of racial profiling as an intended guard against acts of international and domestic terror, we offer two historical examples. The first is from the opening of the twentieth century; the second is from the opening of the twenty-first:

President McKinley's Assassination: In September 1901, President McKinley was murdered by Leon Czolgosz, an American-born native of Michigan, who concealed a pistol in a bandage that was wrapped around his arm and hand so it looked like it covered a wound or broken bone. Secret Service agent George Foster was assigned to search individuals coming to the area where President McKinley would be greeting members of the public. He later admitted to having chosen not to search Czolgosz because he was focused on a "dark complexioned man with a black moustache" who was behind Czolgosz in the line of people coming through Foster's checkpoint. Agent Foster tried to explain his actions by telling investigators that the "colored man" made him feel suspicious. When asked "Why?" he replied, "I didn't like his general appearance." Ironically, it was later revealed that the man whose complexion had so captivated the agent's attention was the same person who saved President McKinley from a third bullet and apprehended the assassin—Jim Parker, an African-American former constable who attended the event as a spectator. Mr. Parker's act of heroism was widely credited with extending the President's life for several days. As a result of reliance on racial stereotypes, the agent on duty overlooked Czolgosz, who despite his foreign-sounding last name—not to mention his avowed allegiance to the anarchist cause—looked like "a mechanic out for the day to the Exposition."

Washington DC-Area Sniper Attacks: During the 2002 sniper attacks in the DC area, police officers were looking for a disaffected white man acting alone or with a single accomplice (the standard profile of a serial killer). After several subsequent reports, they focused their search on white males driving white vans. Police officers conducting surveillance and searches throughout the metropolitan area—including those at each of the multiple roadblocks that were quickly put up after most of the shootings—used this general description of the suspect and the suspect's vehicle. At one point, due to mistaken leads about Middle-Eastern terrorists, the FBI began planning to question Al-Qaeda prisoners held at Guantanamo Bay, Cuba, for possible information on the snipers. Meanwhile, police came in contact with the African-American man and boy—who were ultimately accused, tried, and convicted for the crimes—at least ten times and did not apprehend them because, according to DC homicide detective Tony Patterson, "everybody just got tunnel vision." The suspects' blue Chevrolet Caprice was spotted near one of the shooting scenes, and was stopped several times by police, yet the snipers were able to escape every time with the alleged murder weapons in their possession. Officials were so focused on race that they failed to notice that one of the snipers, John Allen Muhammad, possessed many of the other characteristics often associated with serial killers (i.e., military background, angry, divorced, lost custody of children, etc.). As former FBI Agent Candace De-Long put it, "A black sniper? That was the last thing I was thinking."

Several of the United States' domestic "War on Terror" strategies . . . appear to have been conceived without appreciation for past mistakes.

Paying the Price

In each case, the United States paid a clear price for law enforcement officers thinking that they knew what an otherwise unidentified threat looked like. In the first instance, the U.S. president was assassinated, in part, because his Secret Service agents were apparently relying on stereotypes of what an "international anarchist" looked like. In the second, millions of residents of the Washington, DC, metropolitan area were terrorized for several days as the serial killers repeatedly evaded police, in part because officers were relying upon scientifically-supported profiles that speculated the assailants were white. As DC Police Chief Charles Ramsey pointed out, "We were looking for a white van with white people, and we ended up with a blue car with black people." In each instance, officers' ability to focus on and detect dangerous behaviors (a pistol in the bandaged hand of a white male passing through a Secret Service checkpoint; a rifle in the trunk of the car of two African-American males who repeatedly came in contact with police engaged in the search for a serial sniper) was apparently compromised by the distraction of the assailants' race.

These are not the only available examples of such failures. Throughout the last century, reliance on racial profiling has repeatedly led to national security tragedies. . . .

Lessons Not Learned

Several of the United States' domestic "War on Terror" strategies (such as the post-9/11 attack round ups of Muslim and Arab men in New York City and the National Security Entry/ Exit Registration Program) appear to have been conceived without appreciation for past mistakes. . . .They also suggest a failure to internalize the complexity of our nation's current domestic security situation. While a wide range of "post-September 11, 2001" policies and practices seem to be informed by the fact that all of the 19 hijackers on the day of the attacks were Middle-Eastern males, U.S. law enforcement seems often to have acted in ways that ignore the facts that: (a) the overwhelming majority of people who belong to Arab-American, Muslim-American, and South-Asian-American communities are innocent and law abiding, and (b) many of the Al Qaeda sympathizers detained since have come from a wide range of other ethnic groups and nationalities. . . .

What is more, the decision to focus, even partially, on racial characteristics instead of on behaviors runs counter to a significant lesson learned from one of the most relevant changes in U.S. airport security policy in the last ten years. In the 1990s, spurred by discrimination lawsuits, the U.S. Customs Service eliminated the use of race in deciding which individuals to stop and search and instead began relying on a list of suspect behaviors. According to a study of U.S. Customs by Lamberth Consulting, the policy shift to color-blind profiling techniques increased the rate of productive searches— searches that led to discovery of illegal contraband or activity—by more than 300 percent.

If history is any judge, the impact of this failure to forgo the distraction of race-based strategies means that all

Americans will continue to be at risk of attacks by individuals whose physical appearance or ethnicity defies popular stereotypes about terrorist conspirators. Meanwhile, law enforcement resources will continue to be squandered on over-scrutinizing millions of American citizens and visitors, ultimately because of how they look, where they or their ancestors are from, or what they wear.

14

Racial Profiling Undermines the U.S. Legal System

David A. Harris

David A. Harris is the Balk Professor of Law and Values at the University of Toledo College of Law in Ohio and Soros Senior Justice Fellow at the Center for Crime, Communities & Culture in New York. He is a leading national authority on racial profiling and has written many articles and books on the subject. Harris also writes and comments frequently on racial profiling and other criminal justice issues in the mainstream press.

The American justice system is based on trust. Racially biased law enforcement methods erode this trust, thus affecting the legitimacy of the entire system. Many studies show that black Americans believe police officers are biased. Traditionally, white Americans have been less likely to hold this belief. However, recent numbers suggest that a perception of racial bias in the criminal justice system is starting to cross black/white lines. This perception has concrete consequences in court, where jurors view and decide cases through the lens of their beliefs. When jurors do not trust the testimony of police officers, they are less likely to convict defendants. As skepticism toward police testimony increases, more cases will end either in undeserved acquittals,

*hung juries, or even outright refusal to consider the evidence. All
of these outcomes result from the damage racial profiling does to
the American legal system.*

Beyond the costs to individuals, racial profiling and other
racially biased methods of law enforcement corrode the
basic legitimacy of the entire American system of justice, from
policing to the courts to the law itself. The legitimacy of courts
and the willingness of both the public and the other branches
of government to accept their decisions rest entirely on the
judiciary's independence and trustworthiness. Profiling puts
this very legitimacy—the legal and moral authority that courts
have—at risk. If citizens feel that the legal system acts based
on bias, that the courts allow and sanction racial and ethnic
discrimination, and that judges bestow their legal blessings on
police decisions based on race, the integrity of the system
begins to dissipate. When people mistrust courts, they become
that much less likely to accept their decisions as lawful and
correct, and the whole system loses its legitimacy.

Hurting the Criminal Justice System

In a study focusing on residents of Cincinnati, Ohio,
[University of Cincinnati assistant professor] Martha Henderson and her colleagues found a large gap between the perceptions of blacks and whites in their beliefs concerning racial
injustice in the criminal justice system. Many more blacks
than whites believed that police were more likely to stop blacks
than whites. More blacks than whites also believed that when
convicted of stealing, black defendants were more likely than
white defendants to go to jail and that blacks would be more
likely than whites to receive a sentence of death for murder.
These racial gaps remained even when the researchers
controlled for sociodemographic status, experience with the
criminal justice system and crime, the level of neighborhood
disorder where respondents lived, and ideology on political

and criminal justice issues. Despite the gap, a substantial minority of whites—from 37.5 percent to 47.8 percent—agreed with blacks.

Henderson ties these results directly to the legal system's legitimacy and the consequences that might follow from damage to this legitimacy. If blacks and a substantial number of whites see the criminal justice system as racially unfair and generally inequitable, "they may be less likely to trust system officials and help to co-produce social order; they may be reluctant to assume certain occupational positions in the system . . . and as jurors in trials, they may be less willing to believe police testimony and to convict minority defendants." . . .

Public belief that racial bias exists in policing is more widespread than many seem to think.

Few people could explain the link between the perception of racial bias in the criminal justice system and the legitimacy of that system better than Saul Green. Green, the former United States attorney for the Eastern District of Michigan, considers himself an integral part of the law enforcement and criminal justice structure, and he has great respect for the people with whom he works. "I know the vast majority of law enforcement officers that I have contact with on a daily basis do a really good job. I have a lot of trust in them," Green says. But his own experiences as a young man and the experiences of others that he hears about give him pause. "Unless there is confidence in the system and in the manner in which enforcement occurs, then there's an overall negative impact on the system," he says, "which has to function based on confidence. So much of what we do is based on nothing more than pieces of paper." Race-based mistreatment within the system has a profound impact. "It erodes your trust and confidence in the system," he says, "and everybody suffers."

Perceptions of Bias

Public belief that racial bias exists in policing is more widespread than many seem to think, and attitudes about profiling have played a key part in these perceptions. Consider the recent findings of the U.S. Department of Justice about public attitudes toward police. Americans in twelve cities around the country were asked, "In general, how satisfied are you with the police who serve your neighborhood?" In ten of these cities, levels of satisfaction ranged from 86 percent to as high as 97 percent; in the remaining two cities, about 80 percent said they felt satisfied. Overall, African American citizens were almost two and a half times as likely to say they were dissatisfied as whites. In Chicago, the gap between blacks and whites was almost three times; in Knoxville, it was more than four times.

Other statistics dovetail with these findings. A survey taken in 2000 by the Harris polling organization asked the following question: "Do you think the police in your community treat all races fairly or do they tend to treat one or more of these groups unfairly?" Responses of blacks and whites were almost a mirror image of each other. For whites, 69 percent believed their police treated all races fairly and 20 percent thought that they treated one or more groups unfairly; 10 percent said they didn't know. For blacks, 36 percent responded that police treat all races fairly, but almost 60 percent said that police treat one or more groups unfairly. A February 2000 Gallup Poll confirms this. Among blacks, 64 percent say that blacks are treated less fairly than whites by the police; 30 percent of whites agree—a gap of 34 percent. All of this resonates with the split-screen televised images of blacks and whites reacting to the verdict in the O. J. Simpson criminal trial: African Americans jumping for joy and stunned, disbelieving whites silent and tearful. [In 1995 O.J. Simpson, an African American former professional football player, was acquitted of the murders of his ex-wife, Nicole, and her friend, Ron Goldman.] These differences simply cannot be healthy in a society that so deeply depends on the rule of law.

Polling data on racial profiling show us how African Americans' personal experiences contribute to this divide—and how their beliefs are spreading to whites. A Gallup Poll released in December 1999 asked respondents whether they believed police had stopped them because of their race or ethnic background. More than 40 percent of African Americans said they believed police had stopped them because of their race. Among young black men, aged eighteen to thirty-four, 72 percent—almost three-quarters—said they had been stopped because of their race. . . . Seven percent of whites say they have been treated unfairly by their local police; nearly four times that number of blacks—27 percent—think local police have treated them unfairly. Four percent of whites think their state police officers have treated them unfairly; six times that number of blacks think state police have been unfair to them. Eight percent of whites think that state police from other states have treated them unfairly; more than twice that number of blacks—17 percent—believe this. Blacks see their experiences with racial bias in police stops not as unusual or isolated events. Rather, they make up part of the everyday experience of African American life. . . .

Spreading Awareness

In 1999, surveys of public attitudes began focusing on profiling in earnest, and the results seemed to show that profiling, particularly traffic stops, might be exhibit A on the list of experiences that persuaded people that racial discrimination pervaded the criminal justice system. The December 1999 Gallup Poll asked whether Americans thought that racial profiling was widespread. Not surprisingly, more than three-quarters of all African Americans—77 percent—agreed that racial profiling was widespread. What was unexpected, perhaps, was that more than half of all whites—56 percent—

agreed. The same poll also asked respondents whether they approved of racial profiling. Eighty-one percent of *everyone, black or white,* disapproved. . . . What makes this important is that the awareness of racial bias in the criminal justice system has begun to cross demographic lines from those most directly affected into the consciousness of those who have seldom recognized this problem before.

The Damage Done to the Courts

When ordinary citizens serve as jurors, they bring attitudes about police credibility to court with them. And it is in courts that the damage to police credibility can have real, concrete consequences of the worst kind. In most criminal cases, police serve as witnesses. They have gathered the evidence, arrested the defendants, and interviewed the victims. They are usually central to the prosecution's case. They have information to convey to the jury that is legally required for conviction. And in a significant number of cases, the police aren't just central witnesses—they are *the only* witnesses.

Think, for example, about the typical drug possession case. Although some of these cases involve informants or other police agents, it is usually police officers themselves who find the drugs, smell the burning marijuana, or observe the defendant making a street-corner sale. These types of legal cases are usually built entirely on the testimony of police officers. Therefore, if people who serve as jurors harbor skepticism about the truthfulness of police officers, it becomes increasingly difficult to convince jurors to convict guilty defendants.

James Carr, a federal judge and well-known authority on search-and-seizure issues, says that he has witnessed this phenomenon during his more than twenty years of selecting juries. One common question judges and lawyers everywhere ask prospective jurors during the jury-selection process, Carr says, is whether they would give the testimony of a police officer any more credence or weight than they would give the testimony of any other witnesses. "When I first started out, invariably, we'd have some people say, 'Yes, sure, of course I would, they're police officers, they're sworn to tell the truth,'" Carr says.

But over the last five years, he says, things have changed. Now, he almost never hears potential jurors say that they would be more likely to believe a police officer than any other witness. Instead, a small but increasing number of potential jurors say exactly the opposite. "They say, 'What? God no, I'd be less likely to believe them, they're cops,'" Carr says, "and these are not urban minority jurors. They're mostly white jurors from small towns." People are simply "not giving police officers the credence they historically have," Carr says. While no one has gathered empirical evidence to support this change in attitude, Carr says that it has been "perceptible to me as a trial judge."

Lucas Miller, a detective with the New York Police Department, says police in New York have known about the damage to police credibility in minority communities for years. "It is common knowledge in law enforcement and legal circles that juries in the Bronx are unsympathetic to cops," Miller says. "It is harder to get a conviction in the Bronx when a cop testifies for the prosecution." Miller understands what this means in run-of-the-mill cases. "Many of these trials involve innocent people who must watch those who victimized them go free. Often, in the Bronx, justice is not done because residents mistrust the police."

Acquittals and Hung Juries

As skepticism toward police testimony increases, not just among minority citizens but among all potential jurors, an increasing number of cases will end either in undeserved acquittals or in hung juries. Gerard Lynch, a professor at Columbia Law School and the former top assistant to the

United States attorney in Manhattan, believes this prediction to be quite sensible. "Police testimony is at the very heart of the criminal justice system," says Lynch, who became a federal trial judge in 2000. "If the public does not have confidence in the police, then acquittals or hung juries will become increasingly routine."

The perception that the system is racially biased may indeed play a role in warping jury decisions.

Though there have been no studies to test this hypothesis, there is some evidence that it may indeed be happening. Journalist and law professor Jeffrey Rosen has described this phenomenon in the courts in Washington, D.C., in which a single holdout juror—often an African American female—refuses to convict a black defendant, despite convincing, even overwhelming, evidence of guilt and the vociferous contrary opinions of fellow jurors, black and white. Rosen speculated that the rising percentage of mistrials might have much to do with racial bias in the justice system against African Americans.

Eric Holder, a former chief federal prosecutor and judge in Washington, D.C., who served as [Bill Clinton administration] Attorney General Janet Reno's top deputy and is himself an African American, told Rosen that the perception that the system is racially biased may indeed play a role in warping jury decisions. "There are some folks who have been so seared by racism, so affected by what has happened to them because they are black, that, even if you're the most credible, upfront black man or woman in law enforcement, you're never going to be able to reach them."

Ignoring the Evidence

And nullification by juries—cases in which jurors acquit defendants despite the law and convincing evidence of guilt—has begun to enjoy a rehabilitation of sorts into a respectable criminal justice device. In the twentieth century, jury nullification came to be associated with the odious legally enforced separatism of the Jim Crow South. Faced with serious charges against members of the Ku Klux Klan and other hate organizations in deaths of blacks and civil rights workers, all-white juries would acquit white defendants—nullify—despite overwhelming evidence of guilt.

Now nullification has taken on a different complexion. Paul Butler, a respected law professor who is a former federal prosecutor and an African American, has urged blacks to nullify in drug cases against black defendants. Butler argues that African American jurors should use their power to vote not guilty as a form of political protest and an assertion of black control over the system. Even if the evidence clearly supports the defendant's guilt, Butler says, black jurors should not vote to convict nonviolent black drug defendants because doing so would serve only to apply and uphold an unjust, discriminatory law and legal structure.

It is difficult to imagine anything more damaging to the rule of law than growing distrust and cynicism, failure to believe police witnesses, and even calls from respected authorities like Professor Butler to ignore evidence and law. All are symptoms of the damage racial profiling and its associated tactics have done to the very muscle and bone of the legal system.

Organizations to Contact

The editors have compiled the following list of organizations concerned with the issues debated in this book. The descriptions are derived from materials provided by the organizations. All have publications or information available for interested readers. The list was compiled on the date of publication of the present volume; the information provided here may change. Be aware that many organizations take several weeks or longer to respond to inquiries, so allow as much time as possible.

American Civil Liberties Union (ACLU)
125 Broad St., 18th Floor, New York, NY   10004-2400
(212) 549-2500
e-mail: aclu@aclu.org
Web site: www.aclu.org

The American Civil Liberties Union, a national organization that works to defend Americans' civil rights guaranteed by the U.S. Constitution, argues that measures to protect national security should not compromise fundamental civil liberties. It publishes and distributes policy statements, pamphlets, and press releases with titles such as "The Persistence of Racial Profiling in Rhode Island" and "The Drug War Is the New Jim Crow."

Amnesty International (AI)
5 Penn Plaza, New York, NY   10001
(212) 807-8400 • fax: (212) 627-1451
e-mail: aimember@aiusa.org
Web site: www.amnestyusa.org

Founded in 1961, AI is a grassroots activist organization that aims to free all nonviolent people who have been imprisoned because of their beliefs, ethnic origin, sex, color, or language. The *Amnesty International Report* is published annually, and other reports are available online and by mail.

The Brookings Institution
1775 Massachusetts Ave. NW, Washington, DC   20036
(202) 797-6000 • fax: (202) 797-6004
e-mail: brookinfo@brookings.edu
Web site: www.brookings.org

The Brookings Institution, founded in 1927, is a think tank that conducts research and education in foreign policy, economics, government, and the social sciences. In 2001 it began America's Response to Terrorism, a project that provides briefings and analysis to the public and is featured on the center's Web site. Other publications include the quarterly *Brookings Review,* periodic *Policy Briefs,* and books, including *Terrorism and U.S. Foreign Policy.*

CATO Institute
1000 Massachusetts Ave. NW, Washington, DC   20001-5403
(202) 842-0200 • fax: (202) 842-3490
e-mail: cato@cato.org
Web site: www.cato.org

The Cato Institute is a nonpartisan public policy research foundation dedicated to limiting the role of government and protecting individual liberties. It publishes the quarterly magazine *Regulation,* the bimonthly *Cato Policy Report,* and numerous policy papers and articles. Works on profiling include "Breaking the Vicious Cycle: Preserving Our Liberties While Fighting Terrorism," "Racial Profiling: Good Police Tactic—or Harassment?" and "Ethnic Profiling: A Rational and Moral Framework."

Council on American-Islamic Relations (CAIR)
453 New Jersey Ave. SE, Washington, DC   20003
(202) 488-8787 • fax: (202) 488-0833
e-mail: cair@cair-net.org
Web site: www.cair-net.org

CAIR is a nonprofit organization that challenges stereotypes of Islam and Muslims and offers an Islamic perspective on public policy issues. Its publications include action alerts, news briefs, and the quarterly newsletter *Faith in Action.* The CAIR Web site features statements condemning both the September 11, 2001, terrorist attacks and subsequent discrimination against Muslims.

Federal Aviation Administration (FAA)

800 Independence Ave. SW, Washington, DC   20591
1-866-TELL-FAA (1-866-835-5322)
Web site: www.faa.gov

The Federal Aviation Administration is the component of the U.S. Department of Transportation whose primary responsibility is the safety of civil aviation. The FAA's major functions include regulating civil aviation to promote safety and fulfill the requirements of national defense. Among its publications are *Technology Against Terrorism; Air Piracy, Airport Security, and International Terrorism: Winning the War Against Hijackers;* and *Security Tips for Air Travelers.*

Leadership Conference on Civil Rights (LCCR)

1629 K Street NW, 10th Floor, Washington, DC   20006
(202) 466-3311
Web site: www.civilrights.org

Founded in 1950, the Leadership Conference on Civil Rights is one of the largest civil rights coalitions in America. It has coordinated the national legislative campaign on behalf of every major civil rights law since 1957. The education and research arm of the LCCR is the Leadership Conference on Civil Rights Education Fund (LCCREF), which has produced educational materials, special reports, briefings, and curricula on a wide variety of civil rights issues. Many of these materials can be downloaded from the organization's Web site.

The Manhattan Institute

52 Vanderbilt Ave., New York, NY   10017
(212) 599-7000 • fax: (212) 599-3494
e-mail: mi@manhattan-institute.org
Web site: www.manhattan-institute.org

The Manhattan Institute is a conservative think tank that seeks to foster economic choice and individual responsibility. The institute's Center for Race and Ethnicity (CRE) focuses in particular on the issue of race in America. The Manhattan Institute publishes the online magazine *City Journal*. It also posts working papers, bulletins, and briefings on numerous topics. Recent postings include "Hard Won Lessons: Policing Terrorism in the United States" and "Kiss the Melting Pot Goodbye."

The Middle East Forum (MEF)
1500 Walnut St., Suite 1050, Philadelphia, PA   19102
(215) 546-5406 • fax: (215) 546-5409
e-mail: info@meforum.org
Web site: www.meforum.org

The Middle East Forum is a conservative think tank that works to define and promote American interests in the Middle East. MEF sees the Middle East as a major source of problems for the United States, and it makes recommendations designed to reduce or eliminate these problems. The MEF's major publication is the magazine *Middle East Quarterly*, the complete text of which is posted on the organization's Web site. The site also has an extensive archive of articles written by forum members, many of whom are prominent figures in national and international politics.

Middle East Research and Information Project (MERIP)
1500 Massachusetts Ave. NW, Suite 119, Washington, DC 20005
(202) 223-3677 • fax: (202) 223-3604
e-mail: ctoensing@merip.org
Web site: www.merip.org

MERIP is a nonprofit organization that has no ties to any religious, political, or educational organization. The project believes that stereotypes and misconceptions have kept the United States and Europe from fully understanding the Middle East. MERIP aims to end this misunderstanding by addressing a wide range of political, cultural, and social issues and by publishing writings by authors from the Middle East. MERIP publishes the quarterly magazine *Middle East Report*, op-ed pieces, and *Middle East Report Online*, which includes Web-only analysis and commentary.

National Association of Blacks in Criminal Justice (NABCJ)
1801 Fayetteville St., Durham, NC   27707-3129
(919) 683-1801 • fax: (919) 683-1903
e-mail: office@nabcj.org
Web site: www.nabcj.org

Founded in 1972, this organization comprises criminal justice professionals concerned with the impact of criminal justice policies and practices on the minority community. It seeks to increase the influence of blacks in the judicial system. Publications include the quarterly *NABCJ Newsletter* and the bimonthly newsletter *The Commitment*.

United States Department of Justice (USDOJ), Civil Rights Division
Office of the Assistant Attorney General, Washington, DC
   20530
(202) 514-4609 • fax: (202) 514-0293
Web site: www.usdoj.gov/crt

The Civil Rights Division of the USDOJ is responsible for enforcing federal statutes prohibiting discrimination on the basis of race, sex, handicap, religion, and national origin. To carry out this mission, the division operates a comprehensive, government-wide program of technical and legal assistance, training, interagency coordination, and regulatory, policy, and program review. It also issues reports and policy statements, such as "Initiative to Combat Post-9/11 Discriminatory Backlash."

United States Department of State, Counterterrorism Office
Office of Public Affairs, Room 2509, Washington, DC   20520
(202) 647-4000

e-mail: secretary@state.gov
Web site: www.state.gov/s/ct

The Counterterrorism Office works to develop and implement American counterterrorism strategy and to improve cooperation with foreign governments. Articles and speeches by government officials are available at its Web site.

Bibliography

Books

David A. Harris

Profiles in Injustice: Why Racial Profiling Cannot Work. New York: New Press, 2002.

Milton Heumann and Lance Cassak

Good Cop, Bad Cop: Racial Profiling and Competing Views of Justice in America. New York: P. Lang, 2003.

Steve Holbert

The Color of Guilt and Innocence: Racial Profiling and Police Practices in America. San Ramon, CA: Page Marque, 2004.

Heather Mac Donald

Are Cops Racist? Chicago: Ivan R. Dee, 2003.

Michelle Malkin

In Defense of Internment: The Case for "Racial Profiling" in World War II and the War on Terror. Washington, DC: Regnery, 2004.

Kenneth Meeks

Driving While Black: What to Do If You Are a Victim of Racial Profiling. New York: Broadway, 2000.

Fred C. Pampel

Racial Profiling. New York: Facts On File, 2004.

Michael Smerconish

Flying Blind. Philadelphia: Running Press, 2004.

Brian L. Withrow

Racial Profiling: From Rhetoric to Reason. Upper Saddle River, NJ: Prentice Hall, 2005.

Periodicals

Grady Carrick	"A Police Response to Racial Profiling," *Law & Order*, October 31, 2001.
James Forman Jr.	"Arrested Development: The Conservative Case Against Racial Profiling," *New Republic*, September 10, 2001.
Randall Kennedy	"Blind Spot," *Atlantic Monthly*, April 2002.
Nelson Lund	"The Conservative Case Against Racial Profiling in the War on Terrorism," *Albany Law Review*, Winter 2002.
New York Advisory Committee to the U.S. Commission on Civil Rights	"Civil Rights Implications of Post–September 11 Law Enforcement Practices in New York," March 2004.
Deborah A. Ramirez et al.	"Defining Racial Profiling in a Post–September 11 World," *American Criminal Law Review*, June 2003.
Richard A. Rivera	"Nine Ways to Prevent Racial Profiling," *Law & Order*, October 31, 2001.

Internet Sources

Ann Coulter	"Arab Hijackers Now Eligible for Pre-Boarding," *Front Page Magazine*, April 30, 2004. www.frontpagemag.com.
Nicole Davis	"The Slippery Slope of Racial Profiling," *ColorLines*, December 5, 2001. www.arc.org.

Mike France and Heather Green	"Security vs. Civil Liberties," *Business Week Online*, October 1, 2004. www.businessweek.com.
David Horowitz	"Freedom from Race," *Front Page Magazine*, July 9, 2002. www.frontpagemag.com.
Annie Jacobsen	"Terror in the Skies, Again?" *Women's Wall Street*, July 13, 2004. www.womenswallstreet.com.
Alan Keyes	"Taking Advantage," *WorldNet Daily*, December 1, 2001. www.worldnetdaily.com.
KFI News	"Air Marshals Say Passenger Overreacted," July 22, 2004. www.travelwirenews.com.
Michael Kinsley	"Racial Profiling at the Airport," *Slate*, September 28, 2001. www.slate.com.
Heather Mac Donald	"The Myth of Racial Profiling," *City Journal*, Spring 2001. www.cityjournal.org.
Michelle Malkin	"Racial Profiling: A Matter of Survival," *USA Today Online*, August 16, 2004. www.usatoday.com.
Daniel Pipes	"Identifying the Enemy Within," *Human Events Online*, February 3, 2003. www.humaneventsonline.com.
Fred Reed	"Profiling by the Police: In Search of Reality," Fred on Everything, 2002. www.fredoneverything.net.
Debbie Schlussel	"Three Cheers for Captain 'X'!" *WorldNet Daily*, January 8, 2002. www.worldnetdaily.com.

Debbie Schlussel	"Why We Need Racial Profiling," *WorldNet Daily*, May 18, 2001. www.worldnetdaily.com.
Patrick Smith	"The Hysterical Skies," *Salon*, July 21, 2004. www.salon.com.
Jonathan Strong	"Racial Discrimination: Affirmative Action vs. Racial Profiling," *Right Magazine*, February 24, 2004. www.right-magazine.com

Index

acquittals, 98–99
African Americans
  incarceration rates of, 86
  prejudice in legal system seen by, 93–97
  racial profiling of, by police, 8–9, 37–38, 60–61
  is a myth, 62–70
airport screenings, 29
  behavioral profiling should be used in, 42–45
  ineffective, 25
  racial profiling should be used in, 35–41
Alien Enemies Act of 1798, 24
American Civil Liberties Union (ACLU), 16, 45, 101
American Muslim Council, 79
Amnesty International, 83, 101–102
anti-terrorism efforts. *See* counterterrorism efforts
Arabs. *See* Middle Easterners; Muslims
Ashcroft, John, 10, 20, 36, 39, 79
"Assessing Behaviors" (report), 29
Atta, Mohamed, 44
Awad, Nihad, 79

behavioral profiling, is more effective than racial profiling, 42–45, 53, 90–91
bin Laden, Osama, 7
Black, Hugo, 53–54
blacks. *See* African Americans
border security, racial profiling in cases of, 14, 17–18
Brookings Institution, 102
Burris, John, 86
Bush, George W.
  anti-profiling agenda and, 67–70
  emergency powers asked for by, 36
  on racial profiling, 10–11, 16–17, 20, 79

CAPPS-2 (Computer Assisted Passenger Pre-Screening System), 43
Carr, James, 97–98
CATO Institute, 102
civil liberties
  loss of, is justified by benefits of profiling, 46–50
  con, 51–56
civil rights laws, 75–76
Clinton administration, 64
Commission on Wartime Relocation and Internment of Civilians, 52
community-level effects, of racial profiling, 85–87
computerized passenger profiling, 43–44
Constitution. *See* U.S. Constitution
Cooksey, John, 48
Council on American-Islamic Relations (CAIR), 102–3
counterterrorism efforts
  political correctness hinders, 79–82
  racial profiling for, 19–20
  is a hindrance, 87–89
  is ineffective, 27–34
  is needed, 21–26
  stereotypes are useful in, 74–75
criminal conspiracies, ethnic and cultural nature of, 24–25
criminal justice system. *See* legal system
Czolgosz, Leon, 87–88

Davis, Ron, 86
Dean, Diane, 43
DeLong, Candace, 89
Desi Rising Up and Moving (DRUM), 85
DeWitt, John, 8
Dowd, Maureen, 81
"driving while black," 8–9
drug war, 53, 86

Eltantawi, Sarah, 79
End of Racial Profiling Act, 18
ethnic profiling. *See* racial profiling
Executive Order 9066, 52

Fauchon, Christina, 51
Federal Aviation Administration (FAA), 103
Federal Bureau of Investigation (FBI), political correctness hinders, 79–82
federal law enforcement
　racial profiling is not permitted in, 11–15
　con, 16–20
　See also law enforcement
Federal Motor Carrier Administration, 47
Foster, George, 87–88
Fourteenth Amendment, 23, 53
Fromm, Lynette, 34

Ghannam, Jesse, 85
Green, Saul, 94
"Guidance Regarding the Use of Race by Federal Law Enforcement Agencies," 16–17

Harris, David A., 92
Henderon, Martha, 93, 94
Holder, Eric, 99

human rights protection, 84
hung juries, 98–99

incarceration rates, of minorities, 86
individual-level effects, of racial profiling, 84–85, 86
information sources, racial profiling alienates, 32–33

Jackson, Robert, 24
Japanese American internment, 8, 9, 24, 52–53
jihad, 7
Jones, Dave, 65
juries
　hung, 98–99
　nullification by, 99–100
　police credibility and, 97–100
justice system. *See* legal system

Kaczynski, Theodore, 44
Kristof, Nicholas, 81
Kyl, Jon, 79

Latinos, 86
　See also minorities
law enforcement
　credibility of, 97–100
　fear of, caused by profiling, 85
　political correctness hinders, 79–82
　public attitudes toward, 95–98
　public perception of racial bias in, 93–97
　racial profiling by
　　of African Americans, 8–9, 37–38, 60–61
　　is a hindrance, 87–89
　　is a myth, 62–70

is essential, 57–61
is not permitted, 10–15
is permitted, 16–20
in war on drugs, 53, 86
Leadership Conference on Civil Rights Education Fund, 27
Leadership Conference on Civil Rights (LCCR), 103
legal system
equality in, 72
racial profiling undermines, 92–100
stereotypes and, 75–77
Levy, Robert, 46
Lindh, John Walker, 22, 28
Logan Airport, 44
Lynch, Gerard, 98–99

Mac Donald, Heather, 62, 80
Mafia, 24
Malkin, Michelle, 78
Malvo, John Lee, 33
Manhattan Institute, 103–4
Maulik, Monami, 85
McCarthy, Andrew C., 21
McKinley assassination, 87–88
McVeigh, Timothy, 28, 40, 44
Middle Easterners
fear and distrust among, of police officers, 85
racial profiling of, 7, 9
hinders war on terror, 27–34
is essential to war on terrorism, 21–26
is needed at airports, 35–41
See also Muslims
Middle East Forum (MEF), 104
Middle East Research and Information Project (MERIP), 104–105
Miller, Lucas, 98
minorities

fear and distrust among, of police officers, 85
incarceration rates of, 86
See also African Americans
Mistry, Rohinton, 33
Moore, Sarah Jane, 34
Moussaoui, Zacarias, 81
Mueller, Robert, 39, 80–81
Muhammad, John Allen, 33, 89
Muslim military chaplains, 79
Muslims
profiling
hinders war on terror, 27–34
is essential to war on terror, 21–26
religious profiling of, 79–80

National Association of Blacks in Criminal Justice, 105
national security
ideals sacrificed in name of, 72
racial profiling in cases of, 14, 17–18
is a hindrance, 87–89
New Jersey law enforcement, 64–66
New York Civil Liberties Union (NYCLU), 26
New York Times v. United States, 54
nullification by juries, 99–100

Oklahoma City, 28

Padilla, Jose, 22, 44
Parker, Jim, 88
Patterson, Tony, 88
peacetime, racial profiling during, 8–9
Pearl Harbor attack, 8

police officers. *See* law enforcement
political correctness, 22, 78–82
public opinion
  of police, 95–98
  on racial profiling, 9, 47

al Qaeda, 7

racial profiling
  of African Americans, 8–9, 37–38, 60–61
  is a myth, 62–70
  after 9/11, 7
  airports should use, 35–41
    con, 42–45
  alienates information sources, 32–33
  benefits of, justify loss of civil liberties, 46–50
    con, 51–56
  criteria for using, 48–50
  failures in using, 87–90
  impacts of, 55–56
  is constitutional, 23–24
    con, 10–15
  is ineffective, 18–20, 33–34
  is useful if regulated, 71–77
  by law enforcement, 8–9, 37–38, 60–61
    is a hindrance, 87–89
    is a myth, 62–70
    is essential, 57–61
    is not permitted, 10–15
    is permitted, 16–20
  mistakes in application of, 30–31
  of Muslims
    hinders war on terror, 27–34
    is essential to war on terrorism, 21–26

political correctness and, 22, 78–82
public opinion on, 9, 47
social costs of, 83–91
undermines legal system, 92–100
U.S. policies forbid, 10–15
U.S. policies sanction, 16–20
during war, 8
Ramirez, Deborah, 53
Ramsey, Charles, 89
reasonable suspicion, 49
Reed, Fred, 57
Reid, Richard, 22, 28, 44
religious profiling, 79–80
Rendo, Florentino, 85–86
Ressam, Ahmed, 43
Ridge, Tom, 79
Roosevelt, Franklin D., 52
Rosen, Jeffrey, 99

Schneier, Bruce, 42
screening, difficulties of, 73–74
Secure Flight, 44
segregation, 85–86
self-defense, 72
September 11, 2001, 7
  See also war on terror
Simpson, O.J., 95
social costs, of racial profiling, 55–56, 83–91
speeders, study on race of, 66–69
stereotypes
  are useful, 74–75
  downside of, 75
  law and, 75–77
subway searches, 25–26
suspicious behavior, vs. racial characteristics, 29

Taylor, Stuart Jr., 35
terrorist attacks, by Muslims, 7,
    21–22
terrorists
    are multiethnic, 31–32, 90, 91
    racial profiling is needed for,
        21–26
    con, 27–34
Thobani, Sunera, 55–56
traffic stops
    of African Americans, 63–64,
        66–67
    consent searches and, 64–66
    speeding study and, 66–69

Unabomber, 44
U.S. Constitution
    forbids racial profiling, 10–15
        con, 23–24
    rights guaranteed by, 47, 53
U.S. Customs Service, behavioral
    profiling by, 90
U.S. Department of Justice, Civil
    Rights Division, 10, 105
U.S. Department of State, Coun-
    terterrorism Office, 105–106
U.S. policies

forbid racial profiling, 10–15
    sanction racial profiling,
        16–20

values, debate over, 72–73
victims of racial profiling, 84–86
violator benchmarks, 63–64
Voas, Robert, 68–69

war on drugs, 53, 86
war on terror
    identifying enemy in, 53–55
    profiling Muslims in
        is a hindrance, 27–34
        is needed, 21–26
wartime, racial profiling during, 8
Washington, D.C. snipers, 33,
    88–89
Westies, 25
Whitman, Christine Todd, 64–65
Williams, Kenneth, 80
World War II, racial profiling dur-
    ing, 8

Zingraff, Matthew, 64, 68, 69